AF564862

Organizational Democracy

Collaborative Team Culture

Key to Corporate Growth

Chitra G. Lele

Published by

7/22, Ansari Road, Darya Ganj,
New Delhi-110002
Phones : +91-11-40775252, 23273880, 23275880, 23280451
Fax : +91-11-23285873
Web : www.atlanticbooks.com
E-mail : orders@atlanticbooks.com

Branch Office
5, Nallathambi Street, Wallajah Road,
Chennai-600002
Phones : +91-44-64611085, 32413319
E-mail : chennai@atlanticbooks.com

ISBN 978-81-269-1447-0

Printed in India at Nice Printing Press, A-33/3A, Site-IV, Industrial Area, Sahibabad, Ghaziabad, U.P.

Dedicated to

The most beautiful souls in my life,
My parents,
Mrs. Asha Lele and Mr. G. G. Lele

The names of people and problem statements used in the hypothetical examples bear no similarity to actual people or situations. Any resemblance to real names and situations is purely coincidental and unintentional.

Trust
Each other
And Achieve
Mutual Enrichment.

—*Chitra G. Lele*

If you are planning for one year, grow rice.
If you are planning for 20 years, grow trees.
If you are planning for centuries, grow men.

—*Chinese Proverb*

Contents

List of Tables, Figures and Worksheets

List of Tables

List of Figures

List of Worksheets

Praise for Chitra's Book

(1) "Chitra Lele's book offers a novel theory—'The Perfect Configuration' for identifying and balancing the types of members present in a team. She also provides effective approaches, comprehensive examples and detailed worksheets for assembling well oiled self-driven teams. Her book will help any manager understand the principles that create effective teams."

Jack Zigon, President,
Zigon Performance Group,
Author of *How to Measure Team Performance*

(2) "Chitra Lele has created a thought-provoking book that explains various models and tools that people can use to build self-managing teams."

Mike Pegg,
Managing Director,
The Strengths Academy,
Author of *The Art of Mentoring*,
The Strengths Way and
The Super Teams Book

(3) "Chitra Lele acknowledges what so often goes unacknowledged in most team building approaches: the unseen dimension of "energy" that lies at the heart of high performing teams, suggesting concrete ways to move and unleash that energy. This book serves as a practical, how-to-do-it approach that even novices to facilitating teams will understand and find imminently useful."

Barry Heermann, Ph.D.,
Author of the McGraw Hill Book,
Building Team Spirit

(4) "In highlighting the importance of teams and team building, Henry Ford once said that 'coming together is a beginning, staying together is progress, and working together is success'. These are three important components of teams and performance that are highlighted in Chitra Lele's latest book. By following the practical strategies outlined, you too will be able to have a team that comes together, stays together, and works together. If you can do that, through following Chitra's advice, success will surely follow."

Jarvis Finger,
B.A., B.Ed., M.Ed. Admin.,
FACEA, AFAIM,
Author of *The Management Bible,*
Just about Everything a Manager Needs to Know and
The Classroom Teacher's Book of Management Essentials

(5) "This is a book of wisdom about teams. It is thoughtful and well informed but also highly practical. Managers, team members and organizational leaders will find it a source of clear and sensible advice on creating and developing effective teams in organizations. Chitra has succeeded in writing a book which offers a concise but effective understanding of how to work in teams in modern organizations."

Prof. Michael West,
Ph.D., FAPA, FBPS, FIAAP, FHEA,
CFCIPD, FBAM,
Executive Dean, Aston Business School,
Aston University

(6) "Chitra Lele shines a bright light on the importance of teams and the value of teamwork in our increasingly interconnected world! Determination, connection, adaptability, creativity—different people bring much to the team. Read Chitra Lele's book and learn how to build a diverse team focused towards success!"

Marshall Goldsmith,
NYT and *WSJ* #1 best-selling author of
What Got You There Won't Get You There
and the recently published
WSJ best-seller *Succession: Are You Ready?*

(7) "I have been teaching 'team' classes at the University of Denver for over ten years now and have yet to find a class text that I've been satisfied with; that is until now. Chitra Lele's book on teams has been a welcome addition to the field and an important resource that you don't want to be without. Thanks Chitra for writing such an insightful and comprehensive book on teams."

Greg Giesen, M.S.,
Radio Talk Show Host and Author of
Ask Dr. Mac: Take the Journey to Authentic Leadership
(Bronze medal winner for best business
fable from the 2008 Axiom Business Books Awards)

(8) "Chitra G. Lele's book highlights the essentials of building a performance oriented team and provides new ways of looking at team development through approaches such as energy sharing, team accountability, and the use of a team performance measurement system. The book sheds light on how human, organization, and process factors come together in successful teamwork. Providing tips, techniques, and models for team effectiveness, Chitra offers valuable insights in how to manage team development, achieve continuous improvement, and grow teams into 'mature units'."

Ms. Fran Rees,
Author of *How to LEAD Work Teams: Facilitation Skills*

(9) "Managing teams is a skill we all need to continually sharpen. Chitra clearly highlights ways to empower a team to produce spirit-enhancing results and positive change."

Raj Gavurla,
Professional Speaker,
Author of *Winning at Entrepreneurship*

(10) "The recent history of teams in the workplace has been one of growing complexity—in how they work, how they are structured, how teams work together, and how the team aligns its goals with those of the organization. A great deal of knowledge is now emerging about how to design, lead and support effective teams. The author provides a valuable synthesis of key themes within this expanding knowledge base,

putting them into practical frameworks that should be valuable to anyone who has to create or lead a team; and articulating the increasingly important role of the team coach."

Prof. David Clutterbuck,
Oxford Brookes University,
A prolific writer of more than 45 books

(11) "Chitra's book is a thorough and complete examination of the chemistry of teamwork. The book's attention to detail will help any manager understand the foundations and principles that create effective teams. For those blessed with a great team, this book will help you continue your group's success. For those managers still searching for the right elements for a productive team, this book will help you understand the steps needed to find harmony."

Joel Zeff,
Speaker, workplace expert,
and author of *Make the Right Choice: Creating a Positive, Innovative, and Productive Work Life*

(12) "As a manager, your personal success and that of your business is highly dependent on the achievements of your team. And that in turn, is dependent on your dynamic leadership. Chitra Lele's latest book provides the skills and techniques to build an energy driven team who ensure your business objectives. I particularly relate to where Chitra states that, human factors make or break a team. Working with teams is a challenge and this book makes that challenge much easier to deal with."

Alan Fairweather,
The Motivation Doctor,
Author of *How to be a Motivational Manager*

(13) "Chitra G. Lele offers a finely detailed map which brilliantly describes the nature of teams and how they are built. Written to be exceptionally practical in meeting the challenges of the present as well as our rapidly approaching future, this book can serve as the blueprint for the continuous development and leadership of teams at all levels of the

organization. This is a book for all leaders to keep close at hand.

Mark Sobol, Managing Partner,
Full Circle Group, Co-author and
co-editor, *Leading the Global Workforce*

(14) "This is an energetic book filled with practical strategies for creating energetic, high-performing teams. If your teams aren't what they should be, start reading!"

Dr. Robert Epstein, Ph.D.,
Author of *The Big Book of Motivation Games,*
The Big Book of Creativity Games,
and *The Big Book of Stress Relief Games,*
published by the business division of McGraw-Hill

(15) "Chitra Lele has written a comprehensive and thorough examination on how organizations can achieve extraordinary success through the power of teams. Chitra clearly explains the benefits of linking responsibility on the team (job tasks) with accountability (results): happy, loyal customers and consistent organizational success."

Randy Spitzer,
Executive Vice President, LCI,
Co-author of *Accountability—Freedom*
and Responsibility without Control,
and author of *It's Time to Step Up*
and Take Responsibility—How to
Establish Self-Managing
Teams with Shared Leadership

(16) "I heartily recommend this book because it doesn't just present teamwork in platitudes, but breaks it down into a workable, practical process. Today's employees, at all levels, are by necessity, worker-managers, who have little time for lengthy classes and training sessions. Contrary to some popular thinking, today's workers genuinely want excellence for themselves as well as their organization, but they need a practical, quick study to guide them. That is what this

book is about—practical individual leadership and ultimate organizational success!"

Dr. Twyman Towery, Ph.D.,
LFACHE, President of Towery Communications,
Management consultant and best-selling
author of *The Wisdom of Wolves,*
The Power of Eagles and *The Male Code*

(17) "Chitra Lele has taken a complex subject and presented it in a practical and tangible manner that gives professionals the tools that are needed to succeed in a work world without walls. This book represents a very sophisticated effort at offering solutions to the myriad of issues faced when one is working virtually. Both individuals and teams will find this book as a foundational resource for their business practices."

Dr. Steven Flannes, Ph.D.,
Co-author of *Essential People Skills for Project Managers*

(18) "Chitra Lele has compiled an impressive collection of essential tools for developing and leading self managed teams. It's got everything you'll need to focus the energy of your team on the fundamentals of success."

Jim Kouzes,
Award-winning co-author of *The Leadership Challenge,*
and the Dean's Executive Professor of Leadership,
Leavey School of Business, Santa Clara University

(19) "This book provides a comprehensive model for collaborative teamwork that both team members and leaders can use to improve productivity and the emotional environment of the workplace. It is an important contribution in team development!"

James Bradford Terrell,
Co-author of *The Emotionally Intelligent Team*
and *Team Emotional and Social Intelligence (TESI) Assessment*

Foreword

If indeed there were a "cook book" on Global Team-building, you are at this very moment holding it in your hands.

Chitra's book is very useful for organizations which are either planning to shift from traditional setups to participatory management or are already in the process. Her book is packed with easy-to-remember models and approaches to develop team-based structures. She emphasizes the need to truly empower team members and treat them as knowledge workers and not as mere 9-5 employees.

In this thought-provoking, highly readable work, you will learn the many facets and pragmatic approaches to making your own team more efficient and enhancing cohesiveness in those cases where more work is necessary.

With the skillful inclusion of "real-world" vignettes, you will be able to identify with the examples given and incorporate these same principles with your own groups. You will find numerous universal truisms that have been based on solid research and tested with strong results.

In a unique, almost spiritual manner, your author identifies the "Perfect Configuration". By blending in the elements of Nature, i.e., fire, sky, earth, water and air, Chitra gives us thoughtful insight as to how all of these elements are critical for the success of any team. With an artful combination of these elements, she offers us solid tools in dealing with the behavior patterns to which we can all relate. For example, by looking at the five elements and their traits, you will learn how earth and body are compatible, as are the water and mind. In a similar manner, you will see how the "six senses" are so well intertwined and how any cohesive team needs the combination of these traits. With a skillful and innovative approach, you will quickly see how this coordinative stimulation of each of our six senses has a critical role in working with your team members. These are lessons which we can all identify and put into practice.

Coupled with neat diagrams along with a brief but complete summary at the end of each chapter and very usable worksheets, you will find this book a valuable resource for you and all your colleagues.

Author Chitra Lele gives all of us an incredibly important and useful book. By referring to it often, you will be assured of more effective and efficient work with your own team. Go for it!

Edward E. Scannell
CMP, CSP, Past National President of American Society for Training and Development, International Federation of Training and Development Organization, Meeting Professionals International and National Speakers Association and best-selling Co-Author of *Games Trainers Play* series (McGraw-Hill)

Preface

Team members learn from experience how to cope with daily issues. But the best teams are also able to adapt to change effectively. To do so one needs more than just time-honoured methods, one must understand why people act and react the way they do. In other words, one needs a theory of team dynamics and team balance. And that's exactly what I have provided in this book.

It may sound complicated. Even I felt so in the beginning. I felt that theoretically doing something with teams is less complicated, but practically very difficult. Well, the only way to prove this notion wrong was to not only design the theoretical body of knowledge but also apply it. Now this is where the subsequent sections of the book started to take shape in the form of approaches, models and techniques. After several weeks, I was successful at translating my theory into actionable steps. After reading the first draft of my book, my father, Mr. G.G. Lele suggested, "Chitra, it would be great to support your concepts with case studies".

Based on my father's valuable inputs, it was time for me to get out of the hypothetical mode and take a plunge in the testing waters of the real world. I knew that real-world case studies are the only way to take this book to the next level. Reality check is something that allows us to go beyond the fixed set of rules, to discover and share new horizons of corporate lessons.

Each type of research study shares pointers on specific aspects of teamwork like motivation, performance, etc., but as team players we must also deal with the 'bigger picture'. This is where 'The Perfect Configuration Theory', 'The Six Senses

Technique-based Approach' and a whole lot of supporting models/tools/techniques come into play.

Another valuable suggestion came from my mother, Mrs. Asha Lele. She asked me to conduct case studies covering two scenarios, one where it is a new concept and the other where it is under transition. "Chitra you need to prove that your theories and approaches can build synergistic team structures that adhere to the corporate mandate under all conditions", she said. This suggestion was eventually converted into two solid case studies, which not only made me feel satisfied with my contribution to the subject but also helped me to increase my knowledge reserves.

Every organization has human energy in abundance, but what it may lack is the theory and approach to harness this element of energy. Although this book is a product of my own corporate learning and team consulting experiences, the information shared in here has a universal appeal. It can be used by anyone, right from a newcomer to an experienced team player. Finally, self-directed high performance is all about mutual enrichment and human energy balance, and that's exactly what this book is all about.

Balancing personal chemistry is about exploiting team dynamics. Now, by exploiting I do not mean taking undue advantage. What I simply mean is identifying the five basic team member types (The Perfect Configuration) in order to do away with negative elemental dependencies and nurture only positive relationships by stimulating all the six senses of a team (The Six Senses Technique-based Approach). Once the different types of human energy are in harmony, all the other aspects of self-initiated collective efforts (team building techniques, accountability, motivation and performance, constructive conflict, mutual enrichment and process maturity) follow in order. This belief is not a hollow claim but backed by findings collated in live scenarios. Do I hear the question "Where are the results?" echoing in the background. Not to worry friends, the facts and figures are encapsulated for you all, right here in black and white. I am a staunch believer and follower of 'collective wisdom'.

The book will be useful to a wide cross-section of people, particularly entrepreneurs, corporate managers, government officials, administrators of organizations and institutions, where building an efficient team is the watchword for success and achievement. It will prove richly rewarding to the aspirants of higher positions in the profession of management. Common readers engaged in various occupations will also find it interesting and informative.

Chitra G. Lele

Acknowledgements

I wish to use this opportunity to thank a number of sources of people power in my life that have endured the turmoil and shared the excitement over the past several months of this book project.

In one of my speaking engagements, I had discussed the Perfect Configuration theory in the context of personal transformation and had received an overwhelming response from my audience. Thanks to that instant reinforcement and mental boost from my audience, whose response motivated me to write something related to people process reengineering in the context of team management.

The unique talents of my family members got my mental wheels churning out the right ideas. My sweet parents, Mrs. Asha Lele and Mr. G.G. Lele have always helped me to maintain laser sharp focus on my goals, and I dedicate this edition to them. They have always encouraged my forays into the challenging yet rewarding world of business and management. I am grateful to them for their rock steady support in helping me write this book.

I am highly indebted to Mr. Edward E. Scannell for his cooperation in my academic pursuits, for evincing keen interest in my book and sparing his precious time for writing a scholarly foreword for the same.

I owe my deep sense of gratitude to a series of prolific icons for their willingness to read my work, and provide constructive feedback and expert opinions for the same.

I would like to thank the experts, who gave me an opportunity to apply my theories and approaches in their dynamic and coveted organization, Garware-Wall Ropes

Limited, Chinchwad, Pune. Their cooperation guided me in building useful case studies. I acknowledge the fruitful discussions with Mr. Harish Nandwani, Vice President, Human Resource and Mr. C.P. Purandare, Asstt. Manager, Accounts. The inputs received from these sources have given the book a strong level of authenticity and reality check. A million thanks to the team members themselves, for their constant support and willingness to experiment, which formed the backbone of the case studies. These case studies have added to my wisdom reserves tremendously and I am sure they will add to yours too.

Last but not least, I am thankful to Atlantic Publishers and Distributors for publishing this book. Their professional collaboration means a great deal to me. It is a great privilege to be a part of the Atlantic family. This is my second collaborative venture with them, and I am looking forward to a long and mutually enriching association with Atlantic.

Chitra G. Lele

PART I

The Changing Workplace: The Rise of Organizational Democracy

1

Introduction—'Working Towards a Common Goal'

An autonomous team is the key
To face competition successfully
And it is the sure shot way
To scale new heights of corporate glory.

The last 20-25 years have seen the replacement of 'managers/supervisors' by 'team players'. The reason for this transition is simple—Globalization. Gone are the autocratic days of following a team manager's orders blindly, without thinking or questioning. Today, resources want to know not only what their role is, but also the purpose behind it. Teamwork has grown dramatically in all types of organizations for one simple reason—no one individual has the ability to deliver the kinds of products and services required in today's highly competitive economy. As the world is getting smaller and smaller, it is seamlessly connecting everyone through the internet, due to which the business entities are growing in size and operation, as a result of which the workforce is also being ramped up in order to keep pace with the global growth. No more are organizations an operational unit consisting merely of 25-30 people under one team manager or just one department overlooking the overall operations. Their focus now is on bringing about results by co-sharing responsibility and acting as a global team of very committed individuals.

In tandem with the growth, business owners have come to realize the importance of sharing and diffusing responsibility—laterally and vertically as well so that no one person or group of persons is overwhelmed with the pressures of fierce competition. As a result of which, major market players have revamped their structure in terms of identifying and setting up departments based on the area of business operation and specialization. To be able to sustain this flat structure, organizations need to put in a lot of thought, right from hiring the best of the resources to sustaining them through proper compensation, feedback, performance rewards and required training.

Keeping in line with international trends, over the last quarter century or so, organizations have consciously adopted practices and methods for developing and training people as a team rather than as individuals. They have come to realize that teams are a powerful way for handling matters related to responsibility, accountability and escalation, thereby eliminating glitches like pass the buck policy, ill-practices, backstabbing, etc. This does not mean that the role of a manager/supervisor has diminished in any way whatsoever; rather it has become even more crucial and well defined. Team managers or team leaders have to shoulder the responsibility of keeping their teams intact, of ensuring that the team-based approach produces efficient outcomes and resolves conflicts in the most professional manner. But all this has to be done in a democratic manner. Nowadays, team managers are more often looked at as team coaches or mentors, and not as merely holding a supervisory role. In fact, they have to act with prudence, because through their actions and work, they aid in developing future team managers/coaches/leaders.

The autocratic prerogatives or the 'do it oneself' attitudes have been taken over by collective action and coordinated commitment. Gone are the days of team managers dominating the team scene, now they act as facilitators who make things easier for teams. Over the last quarter of this century, several models and techniques have been formulated to address successful team management. Although there are still issues with team management, but the returns still outweigh the costs.

Due to the various cutting edge communication channels like the internet, remote conferencing and satellite communication, virtual teams have also become very popular in last decade or so. Geographical separation is no more a constraint for managing physically disparate functional units. Thus, teams in the virtual mode are drivers for successful cross-country ventures, thereby opening doors to more global opportunities.

I believe SDWTs (self-directed work teams) are synonymous to real families. Just as it takes time to form and understand the roles and responsibilities of home families, similar is the case with a business or functional family. It takes time to form a functional family and to relate to authority, roles and responsibilities. It also takes time to know and understand each other and each others' roles. But vigilant businesses are becoming more open to the SDWT culture, no matter what it takes and how much time it takes, as they know that SDWTs are the surefire door to success.

The concept of individual performer or solo team manager does not work in today's times. The only way to maximize the effectiveness of organizations is to be able to work with one another to achieve common goals. Businesses today have either adopted or are in the process of adopting the collaboration approach towards problem solving, as they have become aware that no single person or entity is able to survive the shockwaves of the dynamic market conditions. Over the years, employers have come to realize the importance of maintaining a positive work culture and relationship with employees. They do not look at employees as mere staff members anymore, but rather consider them as the *biggest* asset of organizations.

1.1 What is an SDWT—'Join Hands to Achieve Something Greater'

A self-directed work team is a critical piece
Of the business growth puzzle,
Which keeps the business on the rise.

A self-directed unit is a set of highly cohesive, communicative, resourceful and committed people with a laser sharp focus on achieving objectives in a well coordinated, responsible manner. An SDWT is not just a group of people, but rather it is also a process of applying proven techniques to harness the energy reserves (skills, attitudes, viewpoints, domain knowledge, and personalities), to ensure accountability and result management in the most efficacious manner.

'No man is an island', this famous quote is the very essence of team management. Just as our body organs cannot perform in isolation, same is the case with any organization. For example, a finance department cannot run the business show all by itself. Rather the business is run and taken to a new level of performance by an entire gamut of departments and their respective teams working in tandem. Similarly, within each department there has to be a coordinated system of work execution. For example, the head of the human resources department cannot function all by himself to achieve the desired results. The main aim of this department is recruiting and sustaining an efficient workforce. He needs the support and expertise of various other experts in areas like training and development, recruitment and selection, and several other sub-areas in order to ensure the overall productivity of the workforce.

SDWTs are the building blocks of any business that functions in a complementary manner. Leave aside well established organizations, but even startups need a strong founding team. This founding team acts as a mentor for the formation of other operational and satellite teams.

As time has progressed, the tasks needed to perform a particular operation or execute a particular scenario need multiple resources working on it. Individual judgment cannot be relied on due to the bias and subjective element. For example, in a complex SAP (System Application Product) implementation where thousands of aspects and calculations are required to perform the workflow, relying on a single resource is not at all feasible because he may tend to overlook a particular aspect or not report a particular problem as he does not want to show his lack of knowledge. This kind of behavior leads to a negative cascade effect. Here, services of a well trained and highly resourceful SDWT is the only solution to handle such an implementation and complexity level.

An SDWT is a group of people who demonstrate constancy of purpose, by reflecting it through their commitment towards their work, which in turn encourages the top management too. They also live up to their organization's goals by following in the footsteps of their team managers, who in turn, show them how to respect organizational practices, code of ethics and the mission statement. This goes to show that in any successful organization, the flow of the vision is both ways, from the top management towards the SDWT and *vice versa*.

SDWTs are always ahead of their traditional counterparts. They are integrated mature units who fuel themselves with their own collective knowledge, collaborative tools and mutual coexistence. They are a target-driven constellation sharing a strong empathy towards each other. They firmly believe in shared leadership, and leverage the diversity within to keep team members self-motivated.

Table 1.1: The Dimensions of SDWTs

Target-driven	Team members are not merely task-oriented rather they are target-driven. It is the mission that keeps them going and not the tasks needed to meet the mission.
Empathetic attitude	Team members coexist in harmony and encourage each other. The team brings out the best in each member.
Accommodative leadership	SDWTs are about cross-training and role sharing. Everyone is treated on par with his capacity to influence the team agenda.
Myriad personalities	The team is a group of diverse personalities, mentalities, skills and attitudes. This diversity is highly required for the progress of the team.
Self-motivated	The team is highly self-directed. It is confident to take on challenges and successfully meets the goals based on the diversity that comes with it.

SDWTs enable organizations to achieve the extraordinary through selfless cooperation.

1.2 Competent Teams—'Tackle Emergent Challenges'

Laser sharp focus
Is the mantra of competent self-directed teams,
Which eliminates all the hocus-pocus.

As SDWTs are becoming a major focus in the business world hence team member selection is very important, as is ensuring that team goals are clear and committed to. Developing high performance teams is a Herculean task, but once we know what all traits are required of such a team, then the road becomes a lot smoother, and less bumpy. Simply high mental acumen or talent is not the driving force for high performance SDWTs; there are several other characteristics that need to be worked upon for bringing about the best payoff.

No matter what the nature of a team is, whether it is permanent or temporary in nature, the following set of traits is applicable to all high performance teams:

A. Mission Statement

Each SDWT is constituted for realizing a particular goal or objective, which in turn relates to the main goal in one way or the other. For example, the mission of the Human Resources department is to recruit 50 new resources for a given month within the given constraints of budget and time. This gives a sense of purpose that drives them to work towards achieving the milestone within the set deadline. Mission is the most important characteristic as it gives direction to a team. It gives a sense of why a team has come into existence. Competent teams are highly goal-oriented and are driven by success.

Team members assist each other to meet their own needs, while serving the overall purpose of their team. The very nucleus of a team's existence is the mission/purpose, deterring from the same equals to nullifying the existence of a team.

B. Commitment

This characteristic is a child of the earlier characteristic. Competent teams are not only mission-driven, but also go to any length to see that the mission is never compromised. For example, a particular software team is supposed to deliver a work product with a timeline of four weeks, but due to some unforeseen circumstances one of the team members has to take leave. This in turn, has an effect on the deliverable timelines, if the team is not committed. But in the case of a committed team, it strives hard to meet the milestone by putting in more hours. Highly committed teams are proactive in approach. They cross-train in each others' roles and duties so that they can back up their team mates in case of emergencies. Team members are willing to work outside of their defined roles in order to assist their team. They cooperate with each other to overcome non-performance issues.

C. Shared Responsibility

All team members are given their due and fair share of roles and responsibilities, based on standard policies and processes. This ensures that the work is completed with full responsibility and whole-heartedly. As each team member is given equal importance in the decision-making process, his team manager and team members operate on the same level. Both have an equal say and share the burden of responsibility. In fact, in SDWTs team members have a *bigger* say and a *larger* slice of the responsibility pie.

A team manager is more of a facilitator and a coach, who sees to the fact that each team member is given the opportunity to shoulder responsibility equally.

D. Empowerment

Co-sharing of responsibility leads to yet another important characteristic of high performance SDWTs—**empowerment**. Team members are empowered to perform, they are given the authority to decide or act. They are given the freedom to take action or decide for themselves without going through the traditional long chain of approval. This develops an atmosphere of efficiency and participation, as each team member knows that he has the choice to decide the best course of action given a particular situation. This makes a team self-steering.

This also reinforces the fact that the management trusts its teams. Empowerment is not misuse of the power to act, but rather it is the right given to team members to take rational decisions, keeping in mind the end results and the mission of their team.

E. Clear-cut Work Assignment

There is a clear-cut distinction and detailed description of the assignment of duties. Everyone knows what each one is supposed to do and not supposed to do. The scope of work of a well defined SDWT is absolutely crystal clear. There is nothing nebulous about work distribution. The assignments and roles are well specified and have a set boundary, which allows fair distribution of work. No one is underutilized or overburdened.

F. Shared Accountability

The equation of work assignment has two expressions—Responsibility and Accountability.

Responsibility which we already discussed is something to do with the actual work, while accountability is an after the fact aspect. Both these factors encourage a team to take lucrative risks by stepping out of the comfort zone.

G. Diversity

SDWTs need to have a diverse background in terms of skills, experience, expertise so that they can pool these aspects to be effective and create innovative solutions. It is imperative that teams must be the right mix of people, who can find solutions to all types of problems. In other words, a team with no diversity in it is unlikely to work in an innovative manner.

With this diversity comes another important aspect of understanding of roles and structure. Work is assigned according to the skills, yet there is a willingness to take up new opportunities. This diversity is essential to leverage and enhance the team output.

Even in this diversity of skills, personalities, attitudes and backgrounds, the one main factor that is common amongst team members is the 'team mission'. There is no room for hidden agendas.

H. Communication

Honest and clear communication is the basis of fostering a climate of trust and coexistence. Communication not only encompasses spoken communication, but also focuses on writing, listening and conflict resolution.

Clear rules for all types of communication need to be formulated and shared amongst team members. Proper induction meetings work wonders for setting the standards of intra and inter-team communication. Team managers need to ensure that everyone is given a fair chance to communicate, and this can be achieved only when they stop dominating the communication scene.

While communicating with other teams, each resource needs to ensure that the standards are respected in order to establish credibility with others. Mutual understanding and compassion is the key to productive and smooth communication. Just as giving space for the speaking aspect is crucial, so is for listening. Team members including their team managers need to adopt an empathetic attitude while listening to others.

All types of conflict or communication-related issues need to be solved in consensus. Each one of us here knows communication is a two-way flow of ideas, thoughts and solutions.

A recently concluded analysis of 22 years of applied psychological research by Jessica Mesmer-Magnus and Leslie DeChurch has shown that "talkier" teams are less effective. The main point that the researchers highlighted is that who talk more amongst themselves aren't necessarily sharing useful information. Therefore, they're not actually coming to a better result. Rather, it's more important what teams are talking about, than how much they are talking. In short, quality is more important than the quantity of communication.

I. Ground Rules

Ground rules are working procedures and standards that need to be acceded to by one and all, no exceptions there.

These rules permeate each and every aspect of operational efficiency, right from formulating the mission statement to performance assessment and even communication guidelines.

Uniform standardized guidelines are required to ensure that no violation occurs. They are required to ensure that everyone is on the same level. A capable SDWT always lives up to these norms, no matter what. Team members never compromise the rules and regulations for gratifying their personal gains.

J. Interdependence

The very definition of an energy-sharing, self-directed work team testifies for the fact that each team member works with the other in cooperation. No one works for individual performance or in isolation. Every person's success is rated based on every other team member's contribution and success. This unified approach is necessary in order to maintain the fabric of a team. Each team member's contribution is dependent on the inputs given by his team mates. High performance teams thrive on each others' inputs and complement each others' roles.

K. Excellent Leadership

An SDWT needs directional support and reorientation, which can be provided by a team manager who leads by example and not by coercion. He needs to constantly remind team members of team goals and team charter.

In order to maintain cohesion within a team, its team manager has to be efficient enough to be able to mediate conflicts, mentor team members and solve problems judiciously. His intervention in team dynamics is valid only when it is needed. The rest of the time a team needs to be on its own.

L. The Culture of Success and Assessment

With all honesty and sensitivity team members must offer their assessment for fellow workers. Opinion on team output has to be sincere, and also needs to be celebrated if it has met the required metrics. It is necessary for everyone to participate in the assessment as well as celebration process. This strengthens the bonding in teams.

Even when a team fails to reach the required parameter of performance, team members ought to maintain the culture of objectivity and non-threatening assessment.

M. Future-Oriented Focus

Successful SDWTs are never short-sighted. They do think in terms of accomplishing immediate short-term goals, but at the same time they also focus on the future. They consider the future as an opportunity to scale newer heights of success. For example, if a particular organization organizes a training program on enterprise management, then even the marketing team is geared for this program, even if it is not directly involved with the implementation of enterprise management systems. The future-oriented attitude gives team members an insight into future dynamics and also prepares them for the same.

Now we know what exactly goes into the making of an efficient performance-oriented team. Streamlining and fine tuning work procedures and work processes accelerates the team building process. More about the team building process in the chapters to come.

1.3 The Big Picture—'Finally it is about Long-Term Benefits'

Self-directed work teams are the nucleus
Of growth and survival,
Which propel organizations to an all new level.

Fig. 1.1 depicts that teams are the core component of modern day organizations. The large spectrum of advantages that comes along with them translates into organizational level growth. I have expanded on Fig. 1.1 in the subsequent paragraphs.

In today's digital economy, with the help of team management organizations have learned to cope with competition, changing conditions, and the demands placed on them by others. Initially, monetary resources were spent on duplication of efforts, but now, the same resources are utilized with a rationale. Monetary resources are spent on bettering the policies and standards needed to develop great teams. If you look at organizations making remarkable profits, you will always find a diligent and dedicated team behind all that success.

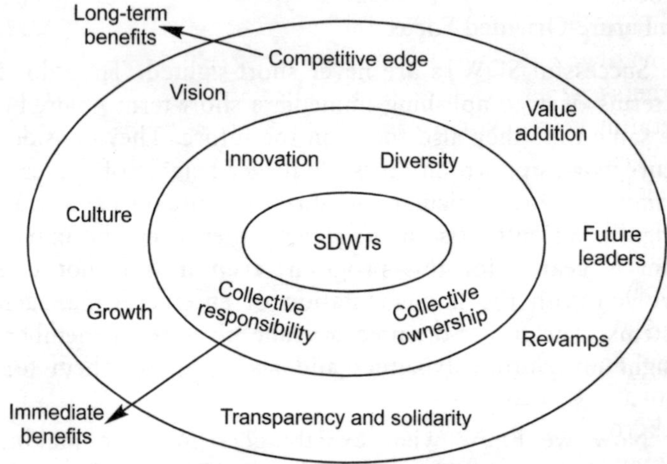

Fig. 1.1: The Nucleus of Benefits

Fostering SDWTs with the right kind of attitude and policy develops good faith and mutual trust, which in turn adds to the multiplier effect of organizations in terms of goal realization, mutual support and shared understanding. Initially, when organizations used to rely on the judgment and skills of a manager/supervisor or any one individual, each work unit is to be task-oriented with no particular goal in focus, but today, that's not the case with the team approach. Teams are goal-oriented and their members work towards the achievement of team goals. Teams eliminate cross-purposes, unclear agendas and unfair competition.

Team management makes each team member more focused towards their work and hence an increased commitment level, as opposed to the earlier way of working in the individual mode, where there was no clear-cut demarcation of duty assignment and accountability. With SDWTs in place, necessary processing and communication of critical information is done more effectively and efficiently.

Unilateral moves of a team manager were okay in the past where businesses used to operate in the stand alone mode. But in today's times of growing competition, of business processes requiring niche area expertise, of global mergers, collective and innovative decisions have become critical. Again, due to these mergers and collaborations, the international business operating laws always need to be conformed to by all parties involved in the venture. To handle this aspect, a team of specialized resources is needed. This means as and when new areas of operations are discovered, a team of resources is needed to handle those operations in the most efficient and effective manner.

SDWTs are a breeding ground for new ideas and solutions. They are the fuel needed to keep the wheel of creative innovation in motion. As people come from different backgrounds, with varying experience levels and perspectives, they tend to look at the business problem statement with different angles and this diversity leads to innovative ideas, which in turn leads to product differentiation with competitors. Over the course of time, an organization is not only recognized for its capital standing, but also earns a reputation for its operational efficiency in terms of dynamic teams. Another important role that a team plays is brainstorming solutions. Especially in today's environment of complex problems, it is always better that teams work on the development of the solutions rather than one individual proposing the solution. Two heads are better than one as they can find out the pitfalls which may otherwise be missed by an overly burdened individual. An SDWT approach is the best route to optimal solution as it is devised based on a diverse range of ideas and inputs, thereby ensuring that the risk of failure is minimized *considerably*.

Having people work in a coordinated fashion and rewarding the same, creates a stable environment and culture for better decision-making. Moreover, it helps to keep track of everything, right from each minute detail to a major milestone.

This aids in assessing the outcome of their decisions and the performance output as each person works in tandem, yet maintaining line of sight focus on his share of the work contributed towards making the decision. This integrated approach of decision-making encourages organizations to take on reasonable risks to implement innovative improvements.

Many a time, organizations face operational revamps, due to which major changes occur, and team culture can make these transitions occur smoothly. They act as shock absorbers as no single person bears the brunt of the competition. In a similar light, success is also collectively enjoyed. SDWTs provide a broader base of support to achieve complex revamps. The challenges are no more a one man headache or just the top management responsibility. The challenges are now shared and managed by all teams, hence resulting in less stress faced by everyone.

One of the most challenging aspects of any business unit is to ensure that all the departments are working together in harmony towards a common business objective. Hence, team management is no more looked at as yet another process or aspect. In fact, organizations now look at it and treat it just like they handle any other core competency area. Due to a paradigm shift in this attitude towards team management, another important factor that has gained importance and focus is training and development, keeping in mind the requirements of each and every team on board.

A collaborative team culture brings with it the three most important aspects of any successful venture—the 3Cs, **Commitment**, **Collaboration** and **Competence**. We can liken this to a family where people have different roles associated with their competencies. The father is adept at finances so he handles the accounts department of the household, the mother is competent with negotiation so she handles the shopping aspect, but they in turn, collaborate with each other, as they need input from each other to execute their duties efficiently. Their commitment to keep the household going, encourages them to collaborate using their respective competencies.

As the business complexity factor is on the rise on a day by day basis, it calls for the management to institute appropriate departments. Again each sub-process is complex enough to require sub-teams within the departments to be formulated. Thus, it is common to have a department team which is broken down into sub-teams, to ensure that an organization's targets are met. Empowering groups of specialized resources fosters royalty and ownership as team players feel assured that their organization believes they are capable of doing the assigned work, and in turn make a positive difference at the organizational level.

SDWTs are a catalyst for taking on complex problems which otherwise cannot be handled by a lone performer. For example, if an organization decides to migrate a particular legacy system to a platform where a modern day model is used, then it is possible in today's times due to the presence of team culture. As this organization has already adopted the proactive approach of maintaining teams specialized in different models, the adaptation is very much possible. This proactive attitude helps in taking up such transitions successfully, whereas in lone performer mode, this would have simply been a far-fetched idea.

With teams taking an important stand in the big picture, the role of managers/supervisors has also undergone a major change. Team managers are no longer looked at as people who have merely supervisory skills or give out hard core instructions. Their role has acquired much more importance and clarity. Gone are the days, when they acted as a medium between the top management team and employees, and gave out orders without any consideration for team members. Nowadays, team managers play the key role of setting the climate of a team. Apart from this, they perform a gamut of facilitation duties, which cater to various aspects of guiding a team and keeping it anchored to the mission. They have been transformed from the role of a mere mediator/order giver to a benevolent team leader/coach. They act as a catalyst for bringing about the success of a team. It is because of the presence of teams that team managers perform yet another important duty—aligning of goals and values. In large organizations, team managers need to align the employees' personal values and goals with those of organizations so that long-term benefits can be realized. More than that, team managers need to align their own attitudes to team members and their expectations.

Another important aspect of SDWTs is that conflict resolution is no longer seen as a threat or a way of degrading others. The team culture has rather instilled an attitude of empathy, where dealing with conflict is seen as a way to improve performance, right from personal to organizational level. The reason is simple: no one is wholly responsible for the outcome, everything is teamwork.

The above aspects speak volumes of a team-based approach. The team-based, horizontal model is the best approach for creating quantum business success. Team management is all about aligning and committing to new changes in order to keep pace with the fierce competition.

1.4 Why have Self-directed Work Teams—'The Payoff Factor'

SDWTs = Peak performance + Organizational growth + Resource optimization.

Modern ways of doing business have changed and are drastically changing the ways we implement team management, but the underlying benefits remain.

Every professional has limitations in taking up roles in terms of acumen, efficiency and skill set. One who is good at accounts may not necessarily be good at recruitment or may not be able to manage it with the required efficiency level.

Again specialization plays a crucial role in terms of commitment and contribution to growth on all levels—professional as well as personal. For example, in an IT development team, if a person who is a specialized certified tester is assigned to coding, this assignment can turn out to be disastrous even if he has done coding in the initials stages of his career. The reason is simple, he may not be able to write robust code for many of the complex business scenarios or may even ignore certain logic conditions while coding, which otherwise, he would have identified during testing because that's where his expertise lies, and that's where he performs the best.

Employee motivation and morale improves manifold, when people feel valued and when their contributions are appreciated and rewarded judiciously. As each person has an undisputable set of duties which has specific measurable performance metrics attached to it, comparing the actual versus expected becomes more accurate. Accurate performance measurement facilitates the identification of loopholes, improvement areas, and cutting down on wastage of resources and processes. As each individual performer is reinforced with reward in a timely fashion, their morale increases to put in their best, which equates to more growth opportunities. This growth is subsequently reflected in terms of the growth of the departmental unit and then finally the entire organization.

Duplication of work is minimized as each person performs duties that are befitting his abilities and skills. Hence, the time expended in reviewing and validating the work is considerably cut down. For example, in case of a manager-driven approach, all the work is rechecked by a team manager, thereby creating space for human error. As it is a one man show, it is highly likely for a manager/supervisor to commit mistakes or overlook important aspects in the work submitted to him, thereby resulting in poor results. These in turn lead to downtimes in terms of resource wastage, rework, correction and several rounds of review, thereby affecting the delivery timelines, severely. On the contrary, in today's times, there is a clear-cut delineation of duties and the rationale behind this delineation is clearly based on specialization. Moreover, the reporting chain is also in place, thereby ensuring that people report to and get their work reviewed by people who are capable of doing so. For example, in a finance department, a cashier works in coordination with an accountant and the results are bound to be proper as the cashier knows the input received from the accountant is correct, since he is a specialized resource in that particular business process, thereby eliminating the loop of re-checking, re-correction and duplication.

With SDWTs, the accuracy factor increases and the gap between expected and actual can be closed, considerably. One of the main advantages of SDWTs is that of eliminating redundant activities. Team members work in unison to address performance and improvement areas. As each person is given a clearly specified duties list and performance metrics associated with each of the duties, the actual-expected gap can be clearly gauged and remedied, thereby making loophole analysis accurate and cost effective.

Rational distribution of workload is one of the most important outcomes of a team approach. It enables to measure the output as accurately as possible, thereby ensuring that the rewards given are as transparent as possible. This transparency eliminates malpractices of favoritism or only some people enjoying upward mobility. Everyone is given a fair chance to perform and progress.

According to participatory research, there can be an increase in profits ranging from 50 per cent to 100 per cent, when organizations adopt the SDWT culture.

More advantages of a team-based approach are mentioned in the next subsection.

1.4.1 Why Self-directed Work Teams—'Beneficial to Both Organizations and Teams'

The flattening of organization structure stems from globalization, increased diversity, the development of technology, and unprecedented environmental change.

At the organizational level SDWTs bring about the results listed as follows:

a. Increased customer satisfaction
b. Improved productivity
c. Higher retention rates
d. Reduced operating costs
e. Innovative solutions
f. Risk taking

g. Appreciate and use diversity

For team members SDWTs are a vehicle of:

a. Personal growth
b. Job satisfaction
c. Sense of unity
d. Career enhancement
e. Sense of pride
f. Motivation
g. Empowerment

1.5 Benefits of the Collaborative Team-based Approach—'SDWTs Reflect Organization Success'

SDWTs make all the difference—
They are the answer
To the gaps in performance.

A well oiled SDWT with dynamic leadership brings a whole spectrum of yields for individuals as well as for organizations on the whole. Dynamic teams ensure smooth execution of work. Over the years, these teams streamline the workflow as they are highly committed to the chartered work standards and operating procedures. Let me erudite how self-driven team efforts translate into organizational success.

A. Teams-> Operational Efficiency-> Organizational Success

When each business process or operational unit is handled by a group of specialized individuals, the final output is bound to be of a high quality, as the respective bits and pieces that go into making it are developed and worked upon by people who are specialized in them. The knowledge and skills are mapped to the duties and roles, which in turn, reflect in an increase in quality output. Over a period of time, positive team management principles reinforce positive outcomes, thus, in a way, teams become self-managed units of performance. This lets the top management to shift their focus from day-to-day operations to more strategic aspects of business. The team culture in a way encourages the top management to lead with confidence and trust.

B. Teams-> Collective Cooperation-> Organizational Culture

As we all know that each organization has its own culture and the essence of this culture is reflected within all teams. SDWTs strive hard to adhere to this culture by putting in their best. They adopt various strategies in order to maintain this culture through collective cooperation in terms of responsibility sharing, mutual accountability and collective decision-making. Another important aspect of preserving the culture is ensuring that each one participates in the process of fulfilling the charter of objectives so that the team culture of performance is achieved, which in turn translates into the organizational culture. Great teams foster a great workplace community, which in turn leads to an increase in the morale of the employees.

C. Teams-> Reporting Chain-> Transparent Communication

Since there is a clear-cut basis for assigning duties, each person knows his scope of the work and responsibility associated with it. Moreover, he is also aware of the reporting chain, thereby making communication transparent. This reduces redundancy and cuts down the response time for solutions and problem handling.

D. Teams-> Workload Distribution-> Optimum Utilization

Workload distribution is another important benefit enjoyed, when an organization adopts the cohesive way of working through SDWTs. As the responsibilities are judiciously distributed amongst team players, everyone is given due credit for their part of the contribution towards the common goal, thereby causing no dissatisfaction and reinforcing individual capabilities. This facilitates maximization of resource utilization, in the most optimized manner.

E. Teams-> Diversity-> Growth Avenues

Since any process is team-driven, naturally the steps required to meet the success criteria of the process are also team-driven. As each team brings with it diversity in terms of skills, mentalities, attitudes, knowledge and experience, the end result is a product of diverse ideas and solutions generated from within. The pool of talents and strengths is one of the biggest rewards that an organization receives from the investment that it makes in team building exercises.

Beyond doubt, this diversity converts into real and significant savings for organizations. High performing SDWTs tend to accept risk, thereby opening avenues for growth, and they also play a key role in discovering new approaches to tasks. These innovative ideas are the source of new products, better working procedures, or even dynamic structural changes within the department and at times at the organizational level too.

F. Teams-> Unity-> Organizational Solidarity

SDWTs represent a solid source of solidarity. The attitude of unity stems from the fact that everyone is treated on par, both in terms of success and failure. There is no lopsided assignment of duties and rewards. This camaraderie maps from sub-teams to departmental teams and eventually to the entire organization as one big competitive team.

Though the team building process is a cumbersome and a daunting task, the payoff from such a task at all levels of an organization is well worth it. There is no doubt that corporate team building gives advantages to organizations on a long-term basis.

1.6 Chapter Recap

1. The focus of international trends is on bringing about results by co-sharing responsibility and acting as a global team of very committed individuals. The autocratic prerogatives or the 'do it oneself' attitudes have been taken over by collective action and coordinated commitment.
2. SDWTs are not just a group of people working together, but rather are an autonomous entity with a sense of definite identity and purpose.

3. SDWTs = Target-Driven, Empathic Attitude, Accommodative Leadership, Myriad Personalities and Self-motivated.
4. The driving forces for SDWTs are a definite mission, commitment, shared responsibility, empowerment, clear-cut assignment, shared accountability, diversity, open communication, unclouded ground rules, excellent leadership, culture of success and fair assessment, and future-oriented outlook.
5. SDWTs are a breeding ground for new ideas and solutions. They are the fuel needed to keep the wheels of creative innovation in motion.

2

The Perfect Configuration Theory—'The Essential Elements'

2.1 The Key Team Member Types—'The Perfect Blend'

Let me begin my theory on a poetic note, the title of the poem is 'Essential Elements'. The following verses give you a glimpse into the 'Perfect Configuration' theory, which is explained in subsequent sections.

Every atom is permeated with Divinity,
Life cannot exist solitarily
It needs the five elements
Of fire, sky, earth,
Water and air, so vital.

The Golden Fire is that creative force,
Which ignites the inner spark,
Illuminates the divine path,
And burns to ashes all that is sloth.

The Astral Sky, so calm
Propagates the message of One—
In this boundless awning,
Doves of peace are in the making.

Mother Earth, our archangel
Aligns with the pristine angle.
Nourishes and mentors the soul,
And transforms unclean into clean.

The Holy Water streams,
Flowing through the conscious,
Purify the senses
and revive life's purpose.

The Pure Air clears evil,
Generates clouds of purity
With the wisps of sanity
By showering the rain of sanctity.

We ought to take in what is good;
Throw out what is bad.
Think of God incessantly–
Worship His glory.
Imbibe this noble message
That God silently preaches
To reconnect to the point of origin,
Only then haloed energy re-balances.

Jack is dependable and a great source of stability.
Janice is totally a people person.
Emily has a great intellect and fine acumen.
Tim is always burning with fervent optimism.
Rachel is always looking at ways of integrating resources.

Do these people look familiar to you? Of course yes! I am sure each one of us has encountered such people either at play, school or work. For that matter, each one of us sees a manifestation of our own innate personality in them. We need all five of these personalities blended well and in balance in order to accomplish our goals in all spheres of life.

In man we see a reflection of the universe, and we are made up of the most basic building blocks of Nature, the five elements—**Earth, Water, Air, Fire and Sky.** Man is an inextricable part of these five elements of the universe. Just as the five basic elements strive hard to maintain balance in Nature as well as in our lives, in the similar manner, the characteristics of these elements strike the perfect balance within an SDWT.

Each team member is a precious resource to be honored, and his elemental traits need to be fused with other elemental traits to bring about a constructive cycle of cooperation, coexistence and collective wisdom. My theory of the five elements of team balance—'The Perfect Configuration Theory' is about deriving this invisible equation of harmony. Just as in non-team settings, if the interplay of these elements is not right then the consequences are also not healthy. In a similar light, having all these five elements in each team in the right numbers is necessary. The main hypothesis of my theory is that any organizational team consists of five types of team members, each unique in his emotional makeup. The five types of team members are:

a. Down to Earth Members
b. Clear Water Members
c. Sure Fire Members
d. Fair Air Members
e. Sky High Members

My theory corresponds to the evolution cycle in Nature, which continues to fill the 'gaps', until the energy sharing circle is complete. Once energy sharing is in form then the energy loops back on itself. Similarly, in teams once the right balance in terms of the above team member types is achieved, the energy shared amongst them then becomes capable of feeding and nurturing itself on its own, *continually*.

2.2 Characteristics of Team Member Types—'The Forms of Energy'

In physics there is a basic law
Which states,
'Energy must exist before matter is formed.'
In a similar light I say,
'Energy must exist before an SDWT is formed.'

The substances of Mother Nature bring about a harmonious balance in the human body, which means this same harmony can be transferred from our character to mould every team's underlying makeup. The most important aspect of this theory is that it is in fact easy to implement as the potential for these elements exists in the mind and always has. It is not something created or developed, all that needs to be done is to activate it and keep it in balance by implementing the tips, tools and approaches shared in this book. Every team member is *unique* because he contains a varying ratio of the five elements, but there is one particular element that dominates his emotional landscape. It is only a matter of understanding the characteristics of each of these elements for striking a balance and bringing on board the right mix of team members.

2.2.1 Down to Earth Members—'Virtues of Honesty and Responsibility are a Must'

The down to earth members represent practical attitude and firm grounding. They nurture and encourage all things that the rest of a team does. They help a team to remain focused by nurturing the team vision with their rock steady support. Once they show commitment, they pursue it directly and consistently until they reach their goals. Members who are born under this element are known to be very principled and responsible. They are the people who first weigh the pros and cons of any situation that their team is facing before arriving at a logical decision. For them anything that is achievable is "down to earth". They always prefer a bird in the hand to two in the bush.

As these team members work mostly based on tried and tested methods to arrive at decisions, introducing too much innovation and new ideas in their work pattern proves to be detrimental. The right balance of regularity and flexibility is essential for these team members so as to enable them to contribute to their team positively.

Their ability to co-exist and adjust with others enables to build a culture of shared values. They are hard working persons and realistic in their approach to solving problems. They encourage others to utilize the energy resources wisely, thereby bringing about optimal team yields. These are team members who through reasoning bring ideas to fruition. Their practical approach guides other team members to understand the reality of a situation and its value.

This element is about being productive and team members belonging to this element bring something new to the table each time. But at the same time, each team manager needs to remember while forming a team, a lopsided assignment of more members under this category leads to stubbornness and rigidity. Too many members of this element type leads to a lack of ideas and lack of imagination. On the other hand, the lack of such members makes the rest of a team reject responsibility, and have trouble following through on a task due to the sheer lack of common sense.

2.2.2 Clear Water Members—'Maintain Laser-Sharp Focus'

Just as water sustains its flow and adapts itself to every contour and bend as it flows, the mind too is fluent, continuous, and adaptable. And this principle can be applied to sustain the continuity of team dynamics, no matter how difficult the situation is. As people belonging to this element are constantly looking for ways to learn and add to their reserves, having the right number of team members of this type on a team, keeps a team vigilant and enhances its expertise. Their calm temperament and great intuitive ability assists the rest to follow the preset vision with strength and determination.

Clear water members possess a human-oriented approach towards all aspects in life, and hence in team settings, this quality helps the rest of a team to adjust itself with the nuances and subtleties in team environment that the remaining team member types won't even notice.

Their accommodative nature proves to be a healing agent in regards to team conflicts. This in turn enables team members to perform in a transparent manner and with continuous efficiency. They are also empathetic to people's thoughts, feelings and emotions, thereby building a cohesive functioning unit. These people think and communicate in terms of 'We'. Again here too many team members of this type leads to disorientation in a team, as these team members are extremely sensitive to others' feelings, they tend to lose track of their own boundaries and identity.

A close watch on these team members is required as their over the top emotional sensitivity can cause damage. Clear water members act based on their feelings and instincts, and too much dependence on these two factors makes them take unwise decisions, which can take the whole team into the depths of non-performance. Too few team members belonging to this element also cause a loss of intuitive skills to a team.

Again here the rule of thumb is the right number; too many or too few team members with such a disposition lead to volatility and destructive conflicts. The same tendency is visible in Nature—when water goes out of balance, the consequences are tsunamis, droughts, hurricanes, and floods. Clear water members need to recognize and respect other peoples' boundaries as not everyone can relate to their emotional affinity levels.

2.2.3 Sure Fire Members—'Spontaneity Keeps the Team Going, Always'

The element of Fire represents passion and zing towards things. Optimism and motivation are governed by fire, thereby suggesting that sure fire people are capable of spreading this dynamism and fervent spirit in a team. Members in a team born under this element ensure that the zeal towards the goals never lessens; their spontaneity keeps the rest of a team super charged. They are the source of mental energy and wisdom.

People born under this element create positive change and see any challenge as opportunity. Their innate energy inspires and energizes team mates to perform. Their wisdom makes other team mates vigilant and enthuses everyone to achieve team goals. Sure fire members make their team mates realize that challenges are nothing but opportunities in disguise. It is here that any team manager is required to understand the importance of giving challenges to members of this element, or else just routine work kills their spontaneity, and in turn, a team's spontaneity too. These team members instill the competitive attitude of risk taking, which is an essential attribute to make a team stand out as a competitive unit. This attitude facilitates every team in its day-to-day activities and in complicated tasks as well.

Personalities belonging to this group need to be dealt with patience and firmness. As they are aggressive, it does not help to be counter-aggressive, rather patience with a dash of assertive firmness is the key to strike a profitable deal.

Team members who are a perfect combination of intuition and intellect propel the rest of a team to the hilt of performance. Too many members of this element result in domination of a team by them. When the collective force of fire is in excess, they feel that they need to do everything themselves, and tend to develop a tendency to be arrogant and control everyone else. One needs to have the passion for work, yet passion over-ignited can cause envy and jealousy within a team.

The only way to control this dual nature of people governed by the fire element is to harness, recognize and reinforce the positive energy in them. They need to be recognized and appreciated.

2.2.4 Fair Air Members—'You Ought to Take In What is Good and Throw Out What is Bad'

Air is the life-supporting element, a very powerful energy source and it symbolizes quick movement. Team members governed by this element prove to be a fresh breath of energy for a team, which in turn brings about upward mobility. The right number of air members keeps a team organized and on track. They facilitate a team to explore its full potential and link members to each other. Their fair mindedness creates a climate of non-threatening feedback. A fair air member needs to keep in mind that excessive thinking can result in lost opportunities.

Air is associated with language and logic too. Team members with air as their ruling element impart a logical outlook to a team and also build everlasting bonds through their power of flawless communication. Here, each team manager ought to remember that though fair air members are concerned with logic and intellect, they are not as much action-driven as their down to earth or clear water counterparts. Therefore, a perfect mix is required to have a good number of both theory and practical team members.

Fair air members are informative, impart knowledge and forge connections. Too many of these on a team leads to lack of commitment and nervousness, as most of the times due to their independent nature, it is quite likely that even if they are amicable, they may not want to make a promise of deep commitment. Team members governed by this element are more future-oriented, and a simple trick to keep them glued to their team is that their team manager and other team mates need to encourage members belonging to this type a reasonable amount of experimentation. Personalities in this category feel powerful due to their knowledge. While dealing with them, a team facilitator and team members need to equip themselves with the right knowledge to put forth their stand firmly. Praising such personalities for their expertise is also very much essential.

This element is about acquiring good behavioral patterns and giving up faulty tendencies. Therefore, team members governed by this element prove to be inspiring role models for their counterparts. Team members who have such a disposition are life savers for a team as they have the knack of keeping the air of ill feelings in control. And when the air element is under control, the minds of team members are peaceful and controlled, which enables them to make rational choices and influence the decisions of a team in the most judicious way. Team members governed by air find common ground and celebrate differences.

Research shows that teams, whose members exhibit a high level of emotional intelligence, come together faster and achieve higher levels of productivity more quickly than teams with less emotional intelligence. When the give and take of emotional intelligence is thrown out of balance, it clearly indicates that the air element is out of balance, which causes fallouts in team relationships. With a disturbance in the air element, team members can become unfocused, distracted, and argumentative; have trouble communicating thoughts and ideas with others.

2.2.5 *Sky High Members—'The Sky is the Limit, It is an Awning of Lofty Perspectives'*

Finally, all these elements if fused together well, enable differing perceptions to be compared and integrated into coherent knowledge reserves, which always keep teams in perfect harmony. The element of sky has incorporated in itself the entire solar system, the nine planets, and other stars and planets. It represents a canopy of endless opportunities for a team to move to the next level of performance maturity.

Sky high members personify energy meridians, they act as pathways that carry energy and connect the various elements in a team. They often inspire others. These meridians can be activated and kept charged all the time, by adopting the approaches and models provided in this book.

They are good listeners and have excellent communication skills. Just as the sky surrounds the other four elements, similarly sky high members gel well with any of the other member types. These are resources that are instrumental in creating space of healthy pockets of interdependence.

The openness in these members provides space in which everything occurs and offers relative freedom of movement, which is very essential for any team to perform. They are basically the source of positive vibrations, and these vibrations are responsible for all the enriching experiences that a team experiences.

2.3 Benefits of Team Member Types—'Map to Team Benefits'

By understanding the positive and negative aspects of each element, SDWTs can attune their attitudes to each element in the most effectual way. To stay balanced, it is important for team members to spend *quality* time with each other, only then team members are able to harness the capacity of their thoughts to reverse negative energy to positive energy. This theory definitely makes teams self-organizing, self-regulating and self-sustaining mature units. Let me give you a simple analogy, the five fingers, from the little finger to the thumb, are associated, respectively, with Earth, Water, Fire, Air and Sky. By themselves they do not project any strong force, but when they come together as a fist, they form an effulgent source of strength and determination.

Table 2.1: Team Member Types and their Advantages

Elements	Traits of Team Members	Team Benefits
Earth (body)	A feeling of connectedness, skillful, practical	Maintains team focus, empathy, a sense of collaboration, alignment of self-perception with that of the team perception, virtues of honesty, dependability and patience, encourages an established team culture
Water (mind)	Adaptable, calm, compassionate	Emotional intelligence, marshaling emotions of the self as well as others
Air (soul)	Affinity, strong and determined, role models, creative	Continual learning, hassle free communication, reasoning, intellect
Fire (heart)	Passionate, force of faith, energetic	Potential is realized, team performance is at peak, high team motivation
Sky (existence/ experiences)	Cohesive, supportive	Effortless team integration, positive energy flow, collective visualization, source of super potential

The down to earth members are like the human body, who keep the rest of a team in form and firmly rooted. The clear water members symbolize the mind of a team, who integrate a team through emotions and empathy. The fair air members are the soul of the unit, who connect everyone through intellect and wisdom. The sure fire members represent the heart of a team, who bind everyone by a fervent purpose. The sky high members play the most crucial role in a team, they integrate all the others. They play an important part in producing healthy team experiences and strengthening the energy fields.

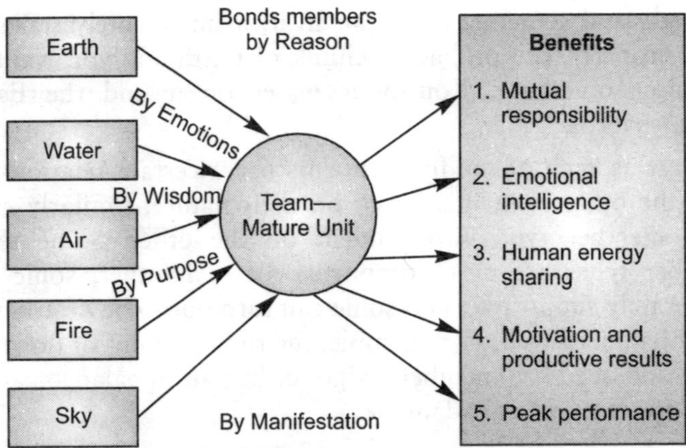

Fig. 2.1: The Benefits of Team Member Types

2.4 The Element Dependency Cycle—'Adjust Deficiency and Excess'

The element dependency cycle—
It starts from nothing
And ends in everything.

The Element Dependency Cycle in SDWTs is about bringing *qualitative distinctions* of a team to an otherwise non-cohesive group of employees.

Just as there is something called as eco-balance in Nature, similarly there is team balance between the manifestations of Nature's elements. For example, if the quality of water is deteriorated due to contamination, then this quality affects the earth element and this process will be cyclic in Nature, until and unless this imbalance is corrected. To erudite further, if team members of the water element are out of sync, then their irrational and aggressive behavior provokes team members of the earth element to also lose their firm standing, and this finally degenerates into clashes. To overcome such clashes, this book has the required tools and tips—the main aim of any tool/tip is about raising self-awareness, the ability to respond to each others' needs and to create living spaces of symbiotic coexistence. Let me cite examples to give you an idea of what I mean by symbiotic coexistence—Let's say fire doesn't burn properly and someone blows air in it, it immediately starts to burn properly, or you have a chunk of Earth and you want to produce something. You pour water on it and the Earth becomes fertile.

Just as each of the five elements has a certain relationship with the other elements, based on their nature, similarly each team member type is dependent on the other. Some team member types are more supportive of each other, some are moderately supportive, and some can turn out to be destructive if not balanced well. For example, the right amount of down to earth and sure fire members is good, but an imbalance causes flare ups or excessive adamancy.

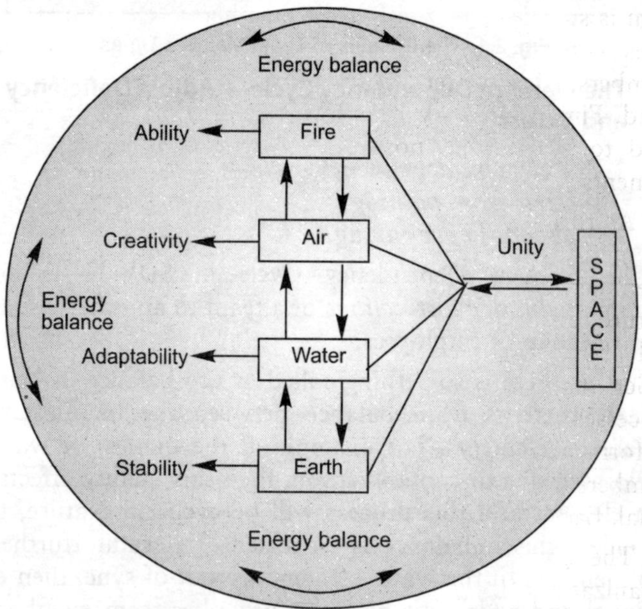

Fig. 2.2: The Element Dependency Cycle

In a stable state, the down to earth and the clear water members are well connected to each other, similarly the fair air and sure fire members are connected to each other. This stability leads to overall integration through the sky high members who facilitate strengthening the channels of energy flow. In a stable team environment, team members depend on each other in an unconditional manner analogous to a mother child relationship. Just as the sky creates air, air creates fire, fire creates water and water creates earth, similar relationships exist in teams. For example, clear water members possess not only emotional intelligence, but also the intelligence of sky high, fair air and sure fire members.

In the subsequent paragraphs we will be studying the positive dependencies between these team member types. Why positive? Because that is the key to all the advantages of team building—performance, motivation, results, collaboration, shared leadership and maturity.

Every team nurtures itself and its values by using the characteristics of the down to earth members. The growth of a team is sustained by the fair air members. The positive energy vibes continue to flow due to the presence of sure fire members. Clear water members bind a team into an emotional bond. Finally, the sky high members are the ones who strive hard to maintain a positive interaction amongst the above elements.

As this cycle is strengthened, it can then further open up the meridians—the channels of collective wisdom and energy. Then, as more meridians are opened, the five elements of Nature can be absorbed and shared by a team to increase skills and ability. Each of the five elements and the persons born under these are equally important, and each of these five processes of action and interaction is essential for a team to perform at peak levels. There is no power struggle as team members are forever depending on each other and all are equal. Each has his own place and function.

The above associations can enable team managers and organizations to understand how to balance team member types and cut down on the destructive effects caused by unwanted associations between elements.

Through this theory, I want to stress the fact that the knowledge of the five team member types can deepen our self-understanding, and give us keys to understanding the behavior of others and the way they impact us.

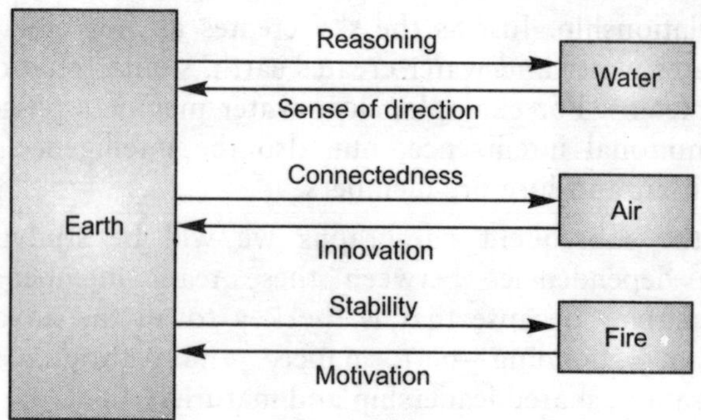

Fig. 2.3: The Dependency between Down to Earth and Other Member Types

As clear water members are ruled by subjectivity, their counterparts, down to earth members bring a sense of reasoning and concreteness to the emotional fabric of clear water members. On the other hand, due to their sense of direction, they help the down to earth members flush away concerns and develop laser-sharp focus on the goals.

Fair air members stand for new beginnings and innovations. Due to their ability of excessive imagination, there is a possibility that they do come out with an extraordinary idea, but if there is a lack of association and stimulation, they won't be able to pursue it further. It is here when the reasoning and tolerance capacity of down to earth members plays a crucial role in helping fair air members to remain focused, get over the stubborn denial of reality and not be impaired by inertness. The fair air members need the support and practical sense of down to earth members in order to manifest their ideas into reality, whereas the down to earth members need the fair air members to apply their reasoning and analytical skills. A perfect balance prevents the crashing of castles built in air and leads to translation of ideas into productive reality.

Sure fire members symbolize risk taking and self-determination that burns away the slag in a team. The uncontrolled aspects like aggressiveness and hostility can be counterbalanced by the stability of the down to earth members. This stability aids the sure fire members to harness their enthusiasm for achieving productive gains. Too many down to earth members can result in stagnation, and the way to overcome it is to counterbalance it with the right number of sure fire members who impart motivation and passion. The right number of both sure fire and down to earth members are needed to realize the ideas of fair air members and marshal the emotions of clear water members.

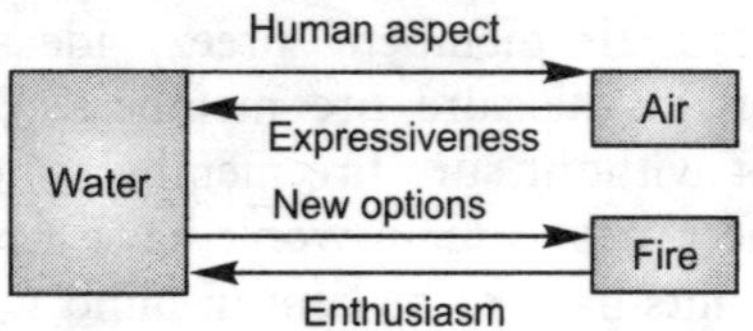

Fig. 2.4: The Dependency between Pure Water and Other Member Types

An imbalance between clear water and fair air members, leads to the clear water members shutting themselves off completely to the intellectual attitude of the fair air members, whereas the fair air members can find the emotional aspects of the clear water members as totally irrational. In the well connected scenario, the clear water members in particular are capable of breathing life into the abstract ideas of the fair air members and making them more human, whereas the fair air ones provide a means of expressing emotions of clear water members through clear communication, which ensures that clear water members connect with others effectively.

Too many sure fire members on a team makes their clear water counterparts overpowered by the aggressive directness. On the other hand, too many clear water members lessen the momentum of sure fire members. The passionate sure fire members may find the calmness of clear water members exasperating, but it is for them to realize that the adaptability of clear water members opens up new possibilities for them as well as the rest of a team. At the same time, the spark of the sure fire members ignites the flame of enthusiasm in the clear water members, especially in times when these team members are experiencing an inner chaos.

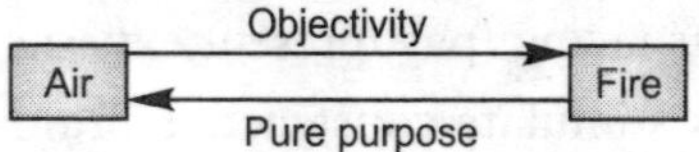

Fig. 2.5: The Dependency between Clear Air and Sure Fire Member Types

Both the fair air and sure fire members represent sources of creative energies. The only difference is that sure fire members can turn out to be more aggressive and act out of sheer impulse. In order to pacify them, fair air members in good numbers are required as they provide a logic/basis, which acts as a constraint on the aggressive tendency of the sure fire members. The fair air members' breezy ideas also fuel the spark of passion in the sure fire members. But again, it is equally true that without sure fire members, both the fair air members and the rest of a team won't have a pure purpose to pursue. These points have to be kept in mind while assembling each team or else there will be lots of smoke (fire) and pollution (air).

In all the above dependency links, the sky high members create space and integration interfaces. Whenever the sky high members become unstable, they are bound to play their shadowy side, and in turn prove to be a cover of deception for a team. Just as these members enrich a team, similarly the other team member types and their traits are responsible for giving a distinct meaning to the sky high members, who otherwise when just by themselves represent only an empty space—a mere void.

2.4.1 Worksheet for the Perfect SDWT Configuration

Team Member Traits

The Team Member Traits worksheet classifies team players into their respective team member types based on past and present team experiences, and the ratings against the degree of presence of the various traits of a particular team member type. In case of a new team altogether, this worksheet can be used after an observation period of the new team members in a new culture.

Team Member Name
Describe how you contributed to solving a critical problem that the team was facing (past/present experiences):
How would you stimulate constructive brainstorming in the team:

(Contd...)

What would you propose to build on the existing knowledge reserves of the team:

What efforts do you make to understand other stakeholders' needs and expectations:

Describe 2-4 accomplishments. Give facts and figures: [use the acronym: DARE

D = Decision (a tough decision taken),

A = Action (what action did you take),

R = Results (what was the result of the action you took) and

E = Evaluation (how would you rate the results)]

How will you turn these statements into positive thoughts:

A. Our team could not meet the deadline

B. The alternative is not the best option

C. Member A and B are not productive

What do you hope to gain in your work: (sample responses—knowledge, purpose, more opportunities, stability, etc.)

Tell me about a situation that gave you trouble and how did you coordinate with others to resolve it:

What are your strongest traits:

What are your weakest traits? What do you plan to do to overcome them:

Rank the team values from 1 to 5, 1 being the lowest in importance and 5 being the highest in importance:

A. Total commitment to ground rules. Practical methods and tangible results.

B. Emotional atmosphere. Interconnectedness and interdependence.

C. Free, open expression of ideas and feelings. Social interactions and intellectual companionship.

D. Challenging and engaging environment. Experimentation is very important.

E. Opportunities for integrating team members and finding team balance.

(To be filled by team manager)

(Contd...)

Traits Summary
Response type: (whether short and to the point responses or expressive and articulate responses to the above questions) Integration level of the team member: (whether independent, dominating or co-operative) (The responses in the columns below are based on the answers given above and team manager's observations.)

Traits	Below Average	Average	Good	Excellent
Member Type—Down to Earth				
Practicality				
Stability				
Reasoning level				
Responsibility				
Trustworthiness				
Member Type—Clear Water				
Empathy				
Compassion				
Composure				
Humility				
Appreciation				
Adaptability				
Perseverance				
Member Type—Fair Air				
Fairness				
Expressiveness				
Cooperation				
Knowledge				

(Contd...)

Member Type—Sure Fire				
Optimism				
Purpose-driven				
Courage				
Risk taking				
Motivation				
Member Type—Sky High				
Builds collaborative relationships				
Functions as an active participant				
Encourages new opportunities				

2.5 Balancing Tips—'Equations Matter'

Remember...

A down to earth member = both the citadel of patience and the swamp of stagnation

A clear water member = both the healer of worries and the whirlpool of confusion

A fair air member = both the breath of newness and the swirl of superficiality

A sure fire member = both the spark of the inner flame and the rage of a volcano

A sky high member = both the canopy of integration and the cover of deception

We as team players are required to focus on ways that let us realize the positive aspects of the team member types—citadel of patience, healer of worries, breath of newness, spark of the inner flame and canopy of integration, and also need to work in unison to keep the negative traits—swamp of stagnation, whirlpool of confusion, swirl of superficiality, rage of a volcano and cover of deception at bay.

To strike a balance between the aggressiveness of sure fire members and the fantasy and emotion-driven nature of clear water members, a team needs to have an adequate number of down to earth members.

What happens if you bottle up air in a container? There will be no movement and no expressiveness. Do not contain fair air members, only then positive changes will occur. A balanced team is about inhaling all the good elements of team building and exhaling the unwanted aspects, and this is where a fair representation of air-borne members plays a crucial role.

Too many sure fire members make the down to earth members find their optimism as an invitation to uncalculated risks. However, the right number of sure fire members is good for the down to earth members since they can bring healthy momentum. Thus, an adequate ratio of down to earth members' stability and sure fire members' optimism works magic for teams.

Clear water members are sensitive to their own feelings and to those of others too, and hence strike associations merely on the basis of emotions. Here, each team needs to leverage this aspect of theirs, at the same time keep in mind that since they are not governed by reason, a team needs to compensate this by having the right number of down to earth members. This balance develops the human side of team management as clear water members are always ready to connect and empathize with everyone.

A team manager and his team need to use their creative cells in order to bring an out-of-sync dependency back on track. For example, to cool off a heat wave, floating in water is a good option. In other words, to encourage the sure fire members, they need to be allowed to generate new ideas by letting them activate their flow of imagination. Then this flow must be stabilized by planting the seeds of new ideas deep in the earth and nurturing these ideas with constancy of strong emotions.

Another important aspect that every team and its team manager ought to remember is the degree of contribution made by each team member type in relation to the phases of team development. In the organizing phase of team development, down to earth and clear water members tend to contribute more, during the action phase sure fire members are the most propelling force, and in the results phase to keep the performance going, fair air and sky high members put in their best.

Properly focused blending allows combining intellectual awareness with a practical sense of harmony, intensity with sensitivity. Once team managers and top management provide the initial support systems for blending all team member types, then the equation given below, always works for itself, of itself and by itself. Every team on its own harmonizes itself without any external intervention.

Down to Earth (practical sense of harmony) +
Clear Water (sensitivity) +
Fair Air (intellectual awareness) +
Sure Fire (intensity) +
Sky High (integration)
= *'Birds of a feather flock (or should I say team) together'*

2.6 The Four Traits of a Team Manager—'Value-Driven'

Just as team member types bring about coherency in a team's functions, similarly we need a dynamic team manager to keep a tab on elemental imbalances. Though we are talking of ultimately having an SDWT, at least in the organizing phase, we need a vigilant overseer who possesses the four traits of trust giver, strong internal locus of control, a source of opportunity and emotional maturity, which let him foresee any disturbances in the constructive dependency cycle and reset it to bring a team back in equilibrium.

These four traits are derived from the forces of Nature—the four directions. Directions exert a potent force in our lives according to the principles of Feng Shui. The four main directions exhibit a unique trait, which we all carry in some degree or the other. North symbolizes stability and security, South provides enthusiasm, East represents new opportunities and West is about emotional bonding. In the similar manner, the presence of a stable, enthusiastic, creative and compassionate team manager is equally important for influencing team formation, functioning and performance maturity.

2.6.1 The SMTV Matrix—'Modes of Managerial Style'

Before I describe a perfect team manager, let me explain to you the four main modes of manager operation styles through the SMTV matrix. According to my observations and corporate learning, there are four main types of modes in which team managers operate:

1. **Stand Alone** (S)—Low value for both team and organization. Team managers operating in this mode are more concerned with their own development and career goals.

2. **Must do it Attitude** (M)—No value for team and reasonably high value for organization. This type of a team manager uses coercive power to get things done. All that matters to him is meeting organizational goals.

3. **Task-Driven** (T)—Reasonably high value for team and low for organization. Task-driven team managers are concerned with merely executing the required tasks and activities, and nothing beyond that.

4. **Value-Driven Orientation** (V)—High value for both team and organization. These are the best team managers to work with, as they understand the implications of both low-level goals and high-level targets. They strive to come up with techniques where team level goals not only translate into team success but also map to organizational level performance.

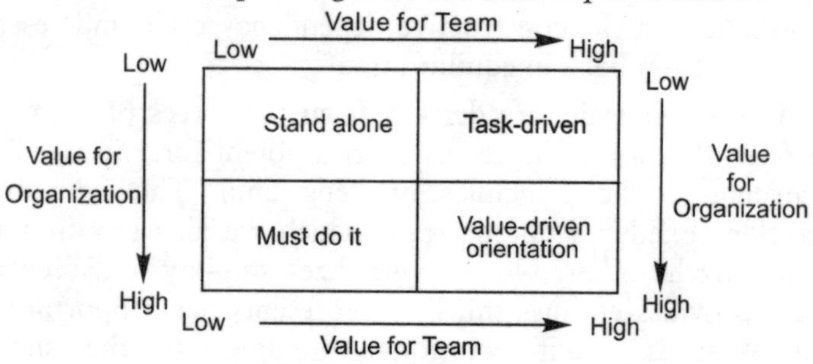

Fig. 2.6: The SMTV Matrix

It is the fourth type that we need to have for self-directed work teams and it is this type of team manager who possesses all the four traits. These traits describe the emotional makeup of the most desired type of team manager in self-driven teams.

2.6.2 Characteristics of a Value-Driven Team Manager—'Optimum Managerial Style'

Except for the value-driven orientation, the rest of the operation styles are not optimum. A true team manager is one who adds value to both his team and his organization. The four main characteristics that make a team manager value-driven are:

1. Trust giver (north)—Trust giver is a team manager who encourages and entrusts team members to take up additional responsibilities, implement ideas and generate innovative solutions. All that a team needs from its team manager for achieving targets is positive collaboration and support. He must have the ability to construct a team and provide incentives rather than just controls.
2. Strong internal "locus of control" orientation (south)—A team manager with a strong internal "locus of control" believes that his team and its team success are purely contingent on their own actions. He sticks with his team to overcome the challenges rather than taking off from the scene. He instills the values of self-sufficiency in a team, and encourages team members to be more future-oriented and plan proactively. Such team managers are more flexible and adaptive to team members' needs and expectations.
3. A source of opportunities (east)—A team manager who provides various ways and techniques for encouraging team members to think, *dynamically*, is a true source of opportunities. He shares his wisdom to motivate team members to step out of their comfort zone, and take on new opportunities of growth and personal development.

4. Emotional maturity (west)—A team manager with emotional maturity is less self-centered, and is well aware of his own strengths and weaknesses. He is oriented toward self-improvement rather than indulging in the blame game. Such a team manager makes all the efforts to align and re-align himself with a team. He has stable emotions, empathizes and maintains cooperative relationships with other team members. He provides a vision to a team, keeps it on track, and motivates team members to execute plans by sharing his experiences.

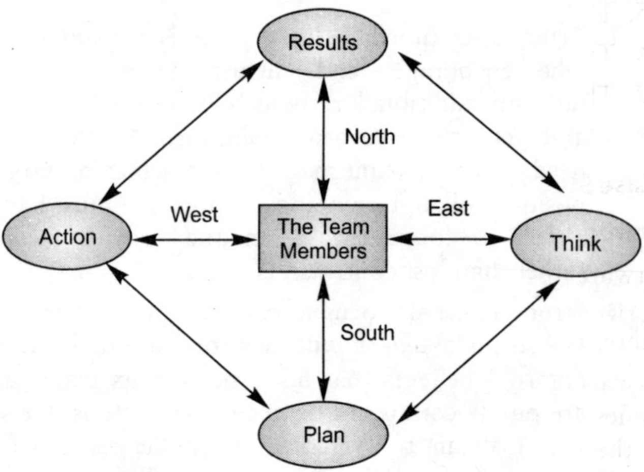

Fig. 2.7: Value-driven Team Managers and the Team

The essence of the above four traits is that a team manager along with his team members strives to maintain harmony within a team. It is a mutually effort-driven process and each is equally responsible for keeping their team on track in all areas of functioning—planning, thinking, acting and achieving results. There is no power play or control conflict, everyone is equal.

Merely identifying team member types and making sure team managers have all the above traits does not guarantee smooth functioning of self-sustaining teams. Through redesign of support structures, team policies, higher empowerment levels and a supportive environment, employee participation becomes "do-able". This is exactly what I have tried to contribute towards through my models and approaches, which design workable techniques to generate positive energy sharing vibes, which in turn leads to mutual accountability for producing the best of results. The various models and approaches that I have dealt with are as follows:

1. The Six Senses Technique-based Approach
2. The Four Facets Model
3. The Quartet Approach of Collaboration
4. The Performance Maturity Loop
5. The Energy-Sharing Paradigm
6. The Collective Accountability Approach
7. The Motivation-driven Model of Results
8. The FACT Model for Team Effectiveness

2.7 Case Study—'Fruitful in Diversity'

2.7.1 Introduction

Garware-Wall Ropes Ltd. was established in the year 1976 by the visionary late Padmabhushan Mr. Abasaheb Garware, in collaboration with M/s. Wall Industries Inc., USA.

Garware-Wall Ropes Ltd. is a part of RBG group of Companies, which is an ISO 9001:2000 certified company. Today, the company is the leading Synthetic Cordage/Fishnet manufacturer in the country and one of the largest in the world. The Company has manufacturing facilities at Chinchwad, Pune and at Wai in Satara district. The Registered office is located in the factory premises at Chinchwad, Pune.

GWRL has a strong domestic marketing network spread all over the country through Regional Offices, Branch Offices, Depots and overseas offices. GWRL sells its products practically in all the continents and over 60 countries in the world.

The Geosynthetics Division is manned by a team of dedicated and highly qualified geo-technical engineers. It offers a wide range of services to customers and undertakes turnkey projects in various sectors like Roads, Landfill Engineering,

Coastal Protection, River Training, Rockfall Protection and Ground Improvement.

The organization is a pioneer in its field and it believes in enhancing itself through various theories and approaches on a continual basis. It was my good fortune to conduct and apply my knowledge in furthering its performance. With such a benevolent management support, it was possible to reorganize work patterns in order to bring about a culture change.

2.7.2 Challenges and Approach

In order to overcome the hurdles related to emotional factors and resistance from the newly assembled team, first a survey of the existing processes and ground rules was carried out by interviewing team members and top executives. These inputs were then collated and appropriate changes were instituted with management support. A series of kick-off meetings was held to design comprehensive ground rules and corporate agenda. The first sign of self-directed efforts was that both the management and team members participated in building the new ground rules.

After the initial phase of meetings and a weeklong training session for orienting the team to the new culture, we went in for a trial run of all the processes involved in an SDWT for a month long period of observation.

Thereafter, we assessed the readiness of both the team and its team manager by analyzing the responses to the Team Member Initiative Level, Team Manager Readiness Assessment and Team Diagnostic worksheets. The inputs to these were based on past team experiences and the dynamics that were captured in the observation period.

From the results we knew what had to be done to get where we wanted to be. The first thing was more employee empowerment and training for the team manager. Employee empowerment is considered to be a key precursor to self-directed work teams. It is necessary to understand attitudes associated with empowerment. These attitudes are shaped and affected by basic elemental traits, and this is where the person-centered focus of the theory of Perfect Configuration comes into play. The main hindrance in any self-driven effort is that of determining and balancing the various personalities. Each team member type and its count were established by using the Team Member Traits worksheet, accompanied with continual observation of three weeks, in order to get rid of any bias element. After this, it was time to correct the negative elemental dependencies based on the thumb rules presented in the theory.

The first thing we did was to have the team build its own terminology and tagline. Each team member including the team manager was termed as 'Collaborative Associate' and the tagline designed was 'Fruitful in Diversity'. These symbols gave the team a strong sense of ownership. Apart from this, several team building activities like an ice-breaker session, team identity building exercises were conducted. The newly formed team felt that they were really cared for.

At the end of each week, over the course of three months, we analyzed the performance of the new self-directed unit, using the responses to the Team Health Checkup, Team Growth Evaluation and the rest of the worksheets in the book. And that is how we got to pinpoint and correct the missing gaps in various aspects of team management so as to enable smooth transition from one sub-phase to the other of the team building process.

Several checkpoints were put in place. For example, regular meetings and overhaul sessions were conducted without fail. The team manager was present in most meetings, especially where corporate agenda was involved. The team manager successfully acted as a facilitator and not as the final decision-maker. He was there to provide organization updates and support the team. By making the team manager a facilitator has in no way demeaned his role, rather now that the team thrives on its own energy; he is able to focus better on strategic issues at hand. At the end of the every fortnight, we revisited and revised the Collaboration Plan and Energy sharing worksheets, to ensure that the human aspect of the business landscape was in harmony.

The most important pillar of collective responsibility is mutual accountability. Here, the Accountability Evaluation worksheet determined team players in terms of responsibility, ownership and accountability, both on an individual as well as collective basis. The rating column guided us in determining the future course of action in case of faulty team member behavior. To control the various accountability areas, the Group Accountability Level worksheet was strictly adhered to.

Right from the definition of team goals and roles to performance correction, inputs and feedback were solicited from team members. No process was the sole responsibility of the team manager. Everyone was given equal airtime and everyone was entitled to build the business agenda.

One of the most important advantages that the team experienced was that of meta-communication. Due to equal liberty, everyone was able to contribute more in terms of work, productivity and creative ideas. Everyone was on the same page of understanding about each others' strengths and weaknesses. Moreover, each associate was given equal level of participation in all factors. By the end of the fourth month, people had come to realize that progressive growth and sustained performance is achievable only with seamless collaboration.

By completely adopting the value-driven managerial style, not only did the team benefit but also the team manager benefited. The team looked up to him as a role model and everyone appreciated this transformational leadership, since there was more empowerment and choice.

We took the required time and facilitation to avoid common pitfalls such as lack of commitment to this culture of change, non-clarity of what is SDWT, lack of continual training and support. It is with persistent efforts of six months that we were finally able to institute the shared authority paradigm.

A great deal of effort had been put into training, and obtaining buy-in from senior executives and team members to keep the process of transformation going.

2.7.3 Results

The change to the self-led team culture brought the results (shared below) in six months:

1. Increase in productivity.
2. Increase in innovation.
3. Decline in average absenteeism.
4. Faster development cycle.

Apart from the above quantitative results, a spectrum of qualitative effects was also experienced:

1. One unified vision and hence more cohesiveness.
2. Better employee retention.
3. A strong knowledge base and data pool.
4. A lot of third party recognition for the team efforts.

2.7.4 Conclusion

Well, this could just as well be your success story. Finally, any self-driven team is about unlimited people power and each organization possesses it. It is just that it needs to be tapped using the right mix of theories and tools. The above facts and figures gathered in this case study exemplify the importance of self-initiated, shared responsibility team structures.

Looking back, team members involved in this case study are able to put in more self-directed initiative on building mutual ownership responsibility. They have learned to minimize cubicle chaos, *substantially*. They have a thorough working knowledge of everything needed to carry out the team's operations. This case study provided a rich experiential learning environment for me too.

2.8 Chapter Recap

1. According to my theory of Perfect Configuration, any organizational team has five types of team members, each unique in his emotional makeup:

   A. Down to Earth Members

   B. Clear Water Members

   C. Fair Air Members

   D. Sure Fire Members
   E. Sky High Members
2. The traits of team member types are related to the characteristics of the five fundamental elements of Nature.
3. The Element Dependency Cycle is a sub-part of the Perfect Configuration theory and it discusses the ways in which the constructive cycle of cooperation, co-existence and collective wisdom can be achieved. It explains how the positive elemental traits of team member types can be leveraged to do away with the flows of negative energy.
4. A dynamic team manager is needed to keep a tab on elemental imbalances. He must possess the traits of a trust-giver and have a strong internal locus of control. It is essential for him to be a source of opportunities for a team and possess a high level of emotional maturity in order to add value to the system of energy balance.

3

The Six Senses Technique-Based Approach—'Stimulate the Senses'

Just as well stimulated senses
Make everyday living worthy,
So do they add value to team work,
Phenomenally.

We are all born with six senses, each one assisting us in coordinating the elements in the world. Only when all the six senses are used, we do find our true orientation. Similarly, in team settings, all the six senses of team members need to be taken care of, in order for a team to sustain itself, and live and breathe its organization's philosophy.

Did you ever work for a team manager who assigned you to a team without giving you the direction you needed to make it a success? You wanted to achieve great milestones, but you realized that you were being set up for failure. It was the blind leading the blind. You vowed that when you had the chance to manage a team, you would do so successfully, and the only way to make this happen is to include the Six Senses Technique-based approach in the everyday team workflow. Proper use of each sense and a results-hungry team is bound to follow.

3.1 Sense of Sight—'Add to the Team Velocity'

Sharing specific and non-biased assessment allows team members to develop a clear sight to discern effective from non-effective ways of performing.

Feedback is nothing but a form of self-learning. A person's ability to acquire knowledge is influenced by the learning environment that he is in. Teams, which are developed within such learning environments, can educate themselves based on their feedback and this unquestionably makes them perform well.

Feedback enables team members to get a sense of what kind of natural talent they possess as an individual. Someone can have an emotional orientation; someone else can be more technical. Every team member has at least one strong talent with varying levels of other talents. Assessment and feedback provides a sense of sight and this sense of sight delineates the various types of talent, which a team can leverage to balance itself out.

3.1.1 Feedback Ownership—'Remove Learning Roadblocks'

Rather than only giving feedback to a team, it is always more beneficial to let a team evaluate and process its own feedback. This way they feel more reassured that they are not only given feedback, but also given space to analyze and reflect on their performance and what needs to be done to improve it. Ownership of feedback is something that encourages every team and its members to genuinely improve. It charges them to channelize the feedback they are given into action.

3.1.2 The Personal Level—'Improve upon Self-performance'

Individual level feedback interviews are the best way to create a platform for healthy dialog. These feedback sessions are not a mere dialog, but rather they are pre-planned sessions to ensure that a team member sees clearly how his career is going to shape up, and what is the roadmap that he needs to follow in order to meet both his personal goals and team growth requirements.

The above ways further strengthen the sense of sight, which gives a definite direction while designing team development programs. They also provide a 'bird's eye view' of a team's performance, which can be used for the appraisal process while determining appraisal ratings, personal strengths and problem areas of team members. They also provide a sense of sight of those individuals who have the potential to operate at the next level. Such tools also provide insight about team functioning, direction, working relationships, culture, communications, etc.

3.2 Sense of Sound—'Recognize, Reward and Reinforce'

Having regular sessions of team recognition and hearing words of appreciation keeps a team fueled. Every person in your team is moved by some combination of internal and external motivators. What works for one employee may actually not work for another employee. Your motivational tool kit needs to be revisited and revised regularly, if you want to keep each and every team member engaged.

Everyone wants to feel important and be considered as an enterprising professional. To do this, we seek out people with similar interest. A team is a social group; team members with similar interests tend to sustain this group, while the rest are more inclined to reject such setups. The most powerful technique of ensuring that everyone feels valued is to assign equal responsibility to all. Another advantage of doing so is that teams with responsibility learn faster than those who only follow orders. Responsibility is a kind of team motivation, but apart from this, a team also needs to hear words of encouragement, which caters to their sense of sound.

3.2.1 Constant Correspondence—'Constant is the Keyword Here'

Constant correspondence is an absolute essential, whether it is in the form of an appreciative pat, words of praise or a letter of recognition, the keyword here is 'constant'.

Obviously, the more you praise your team members, the more they are going to feel motivated to achieve greater accomplishments in the future.

3.2.2 Peer-to-peer Recognition—'No Room for Managerial Favoritism'

Top management sponsored recognition is necessary, but what is even more important is peer participation in expressing praise for each other. This way each team member knows for certain that his words and suggestions also matter. Peer recognition carries the personal touch that is absent in a management sponsored recognition system.

There can be suggestion boxes or a suggestion e-mail, where team members can register their opinions and great ideas, which then can be appreciated out in the open or rewarded in kind. Apart from this, a team can also exchange positive words through thank you notes, traveling trophies, reading out appreciation profiles of each other in informal team meetings.

In creating team-owned recognition, a team needs to constantly develop ways to express appreciation for their co-workers, who make a difference in everyday work life.

3.2.3 Praise out in the Open—'Make Each Team Member Feel Like a Winner'

Praise is something to be shared out in the open. Showing appreciation in front of other team members, in formal meetings and praising a team in front of the management particularly, boosts the team morale a lot. It encourages team members to put in more efforts to earn this public praise.

The above techniques give the SDWTs a concrete sense of accomplishment and where they fit in their organization.

3.3 Sense of Feel—'Stimulus Leads to Satisfaction and Success'

Motivation in terms of bonus and rewards is effective. But more important is 'psychological' motivation which makes a team feel valued and wanted. Motivation is achieved when the need of admiration for team members' achievements is fulfilled, and this is directly linked to the sense of sound. Let's open the motivation chest to find out what kind of techniques can be used to cater to the sense of feel of a team.

3.3.1 Gracious Workplace—'Achieve Outstanding Team Loyalty'

Employee motivation is not limited to monetary compensation or job-related enhancements, but it is also related to enquiring about a team member's personal interests, family and aspirations. Every team manager needs to assist his team in creating such a family-oriented team culture in order to make team members feel cared for. Every organization needs to remember and cater to both the personal and professional lives of team members. Just as it supports team success celebration, in the same manner, it is essential that special occasions like member birthdays are also celebrated.

By creating spaces where team members can voice their opinions, organizations in a way replace fragmentation with cooperation. By allowing each team member to have his own space, enables a team to become free from mistrust, and encourages all team members to collaborate to form and realize a shared vision.

3.3.2 Ideas—'And More Ideas'

Team members along with their team manager, need to come up with new ideas to make them feel motivated on a continual basis. Soliciting maximum number of ideas from team members is very essential. In combination with team member ideas, there are several little things that a team manager can do to make employees feel encouraged. Team members can be asked to attend meetings in place of their team manager when he is not available or be given gift certificates for conforming to ground rules.

Other activities like in-house sessions for team member skills enhancement, flexi-timings, creating a hall of fame wall with names and photos of outstanding team members, team lunch parties not only make a team feel motivated, but also foster a whole lot of team building skills.

3.3.3 Opportunities—'Knowledge-sharing Leads to Team Involvement'

People who have opportunity to share knowledge and learn more feel they are a part of a team. Team members want to impress each other with their ability to contribute valuable information. Repetitive tasks kill the desire to learn. There is always a better way of doing a task, including repetitive ones, and better ways are found with team member participation.

Challenges motivate people to learn and the desire to learn is based on the opportunity for challenges.

3.4 Sense of Smell—'Egos Need to be Put on the Back Burner'

Teams are comprised of human factors that are highly sensitive. Thus, team managers along with executive sponsor need to ensure that the team atmosphere is free from foul play. Office politics isn't avoidable, but there needs to be a system in place to cope with politics. The right level of conflict can be healthy and keeps people on their toes, but too much of office politics leads to poor performance and dissatisfaction with the work environment.

3.4.1 Reprimand Immature Behavior—'Team Discipline is the Only Way to Erase Reactionary Behavior'

The first sign of a clash among team members and then members taking it to their team manager or the sponsor, and their team manager or sponsor entertaining the tail tattling bandwagon only reinforces immaturity. The executive component of a team needs to let team members know that such immature behavior is not acceptable. Name calling and finger pointing is something that an organization shouldn't tolerate. Each and every team manager himself needs to lead his team by setting a fine example of professional behavior, only then team members show the willingness to sort out genuine incompatibilities, and not indulge in cut throat attitudes and hidden motives.

3.4.2 Stand for Yourself—'Grow Through the Process of Self-directed Efforts'

On the one hand, there are people who continue to give their best without indulging in the game of dirty politics, whereas on the other hand, there are others who use a toady plot to make you look bad in front of others. The best way to deal with such a situation is to confront them in front of the rest of a team in a professional manner. This way you not only earn respect from your colleagues, but also succeed in nullifying the baseless stands made by the anti-faction.

3.4.3 Unnecessary Intervention—'Stay Away from Cubicle Chaos'

The best way to avoid politics is to stay away from issues that don't relate to you directly. Team members need to understand that by adhering to such controlled behavior, they are not contributing to the grapevine process and hence discouraging the acts of wrong doers.

Office politics in a way can enhance one's career, but not at the cost of overlooking true talent. The above techniques ensure that the setup is free from the stench of peer pits. They let team members to breathe (perform) in a free, uninhibited culture, where diligence and sincerity are recognized and rewarded, and ulterior tactics are discouraged.

The above techniques ascertain the fact that organizations want team members to spend far less time on political aspects of work and pay laser-focused attention to their jobs.

3.5 Sense of Taste—'Need to Understand Each Other More'

Every SDWT has an emotional fabric and to maintain it, each and every team member must be able to strike the right chords of mutual understanding. Only then a team is able to touch the peak of perfection and taste sweet success.

3.5.1 Building Emotional Equity—'Integrate Branding Efforts'

There are several ways of achieving emotional equity. The most important one is that of creating a sense of common purpose. The most important aspects of any team effort are that of planning, evaluation and implementation. Once people realize that some team members are good at planning, some at evaluation and rest at implementation, then team members are able to truly forge emotional bonds on the one hand and hone self-leadership skills of a team as a whole on the other hand.

Organizations need to realize that emotional equity adds to the whole process of brand building. The meaningful differences within a team set an organization's brand apart. Neither the logo nor tagline creates the brand name, but it is the emotional equity that does. Teams in your organization are the real marketing department.

3.5.2 The Don'ts—'Eliminate Negative Behavior'

The only way to touch someone positively and eliminate the taste of bitterness is through positive behavior and actions. The 5 don'ts aid each team member to be a self-determiner, and in turn add to the self-directed, self-managed factor of a team as a whole.

1. Don't over rely on outside guidance to effectuate your growth needs, rather fulfill your needs from within.
2. Don't project self-diminishment, rather project reliance and stability.
3. Don't look out for unnecessary encouragement from others, rather you build it within yourself and then share it with others.
4. Don't blame yourself or the others for causes of failure, rather look for solutions for the failure.
5. Don't give in to unnecessary peer pressure or bureaucratic interference, rather rev-up inner confidence to stand up for your needs and goals.

3.6 Sense of Self-awareness—'Mental Focus is the Key'

The sixth sense is the sense of equilibrium and mental focus. It is in fact essential to everything that a team does. It provides a sense of timing and coordination. It is about emotional bonding between team members. All the above five senses strengthen this sense. This sense maintains awareness of being or not being on track.

3.6.1 The Right Level of Guidance—'Adequate Space and Scope for Self-direction'

The state of balance is about building energy smart teams. One gets better results from thoughtful and considered guidance than by telling a team specifically what to do and how to do it, the 'spoon feeding' approach is not at all workable.

Team members need to be given their own space to operate well and analyze their work patterns. The required level of guidance combined with an environment of openness and transparency adds value to the team capability. Let them have the freedom to direct themselves and give them the flexibility to change, improve and deprecate work patterns, in order to meet the demands placed on a team.

3.6.2 Collaborative Dashboard—'Keep a Tab on Collaborative Development at All Levels'

Collaborative dashboard or in simple terms integration hub is nothing but the usage of apt monitoring tools and interfaces for collaboration, not only within a team, but also to ensure that team members impact their organization even in cross-cutting and multi-team initiatives. By letting them use these tools to enhance their sense of connection at all levels of their organization, instills in them a strong sense of stability and balance.

The above methods deliver insight into team performance, which in turn let a team to proactively manage itself. They enable team members to increase group accountability, reduce risks, and meet business goals on time and within the budget constraints.

SDWTs are not merely about identifying star performers and solely relying on them, rather successful teams are those units who collaborate and pull together varied skills to pull off outstanding performance feats. Each sense is an information processing hub, which helps team members to know what is going right for them and what is not. The management needs to institutionalize various techniques and tools to keep all these senses satisfied in order to bring the best of team results to the fore.

Sense of Sight is about team feedback and improvement.

Sense of Feel is about team satisfaction and loyalty.

Sense of Sound is about team recognition and reinforcement.

Sense of Smell is about team discipline and strong values.

Sense of Taste is about emotional equity and positive dynamics.

Sense of Self-awareness is about collective mental focus.

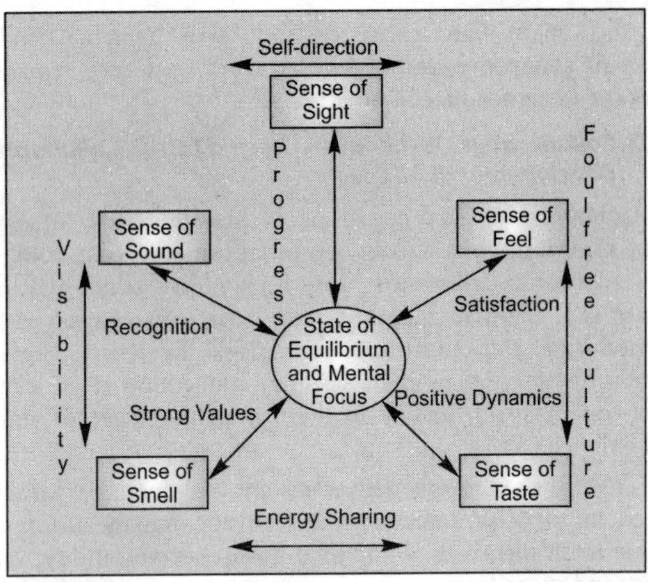

Fig. 3.1: The Six Senses Technique-based Approach

3.7 Chapter Recap

The Six Senses Technique-based approach emphasizes the importance of keeping all the six senses of team members constantly stimulated.

This approach is synonymous to the common things that each one of us does in our personal lives to keep us going. If we apply these very principles to the professional setting as well, then a complete, balanced life is not a far away dream any longer. When all the above senses receive the *right* level of stimulus, they are bound to operate at their peak levels, be it in the personal setting or in the professional team work environment.

4

The Phases of Team Development—'The OAR Phases of Team Growth'

Building your self-directed work team
Means building your business.
Team members are no longer mere working robots;
They too add value with all zealousness.

Just as we humans undergo a cycle of development, similarly teams too undergo a development life cycle of their own. Just as we need training and support to perform efficiently at all phases of the life cycle, the same applies to team members too. Time and effort are required to move through the various team development phases, but it is well worth the time and efforts, as the benefits derived are substantial in nature and long lasting.

Checkpoints in the form of meetings, mentoring sessions, status review and training at regular intervals, keep the SDWTs on track and minimize the frustration experienced by them, considerably. The success of each phase of the development life cycle is reasonably dependent on the skills of its team manager. The facilitation of transition from one phase to the other is one of the most important duties of a team manager. It is essential for every team manager to know what the various growth phases of a developing team are, and also know how best to move a team through these phases. He needs to realize that facilitation is not about bossing around, but it is about the right level of support.

The team life cycle is all about regrouping and refocusing, in line with any changes in the team dynamics.

4.1 Organizing Phase—'Ad-hoc and Functional Processes'

The organizing phase is mainly focused on a situational analysis to determine the importance of a team to its organization, the urgency with which a team must act, and the level of power, influence and support a team will experience—a team tries to figure out what they are "really getting into" and what challenges lie ahead. In the beginning the team dynamics are quite chaotic and ad-hoc, steadily they become somewhat manageable and repeatable.

This phase requires high levels of participation, to maximize team member ownership and commitment to the team's mission, goals and strategies—only then a team by itself can handle its mission, goals, strategies and structure well. Only then these milestones turn a "collection of individuals" into a "team" with a clear purpose and direction through the various phases of team maturity.

The organizing phase consists of two sub-phases:

A. Growth through speculation
B. Growth through conflict

4.1.1 Growth Through Speculation—'Getting to Know Each Other'

Do you remember the first day of your job, to be more precise the first day of work in a new team? If yes, then you will also recall the air of confusion and nervousness. This is where people are in the process of getting to know each other. They are a mixed bag of emotions—nervous and excited as well.

In this sub-phase, more than the actual nature of work people are keen to know about their roles and where exactly they fit into a team. They are also eager to learn about the main mission which has brought them all together. At the same time, each one is interested in knowing the other's role and responsibilities. The answers to these questions aid each team member to figure out what is his exact standing in a team.

Even before teamwork is officially initiated, team members indulge in heavy speculation and guesstimates about a team and its dynamics. There is a lot of confusion regarding the goals, tasks and responsibilities. It is in this sub-phase that team members get their first glimpse of what opportunities and threats they are going to face as a team.

Depending on the complexity of the project, this sub-phase can last from anywhere between a few days to a few weeks.

A whole lot of questions crop up in every team member's mind:

A. What other team members are like?
B. Will they accept me?
C. Is the work going to be challenging enough?
D. Will I get my due share of credit?
E. Will the team have competent leadership?
F. Is the management benevolent?
G. What is the growth potential?

4.1.2 How to Facilitate Sub-phase 1

As I said earlier, individuals draw their own conclusions about a team, which most of the times is nothing but a speculative guess. These guesstimates can lead to future problems, if not cleared in this sub-phase itself. It is here, where a team manager steps in to clarify all the doubts. It is the foremost duty of each and every team manager to get all team members on a common level of understanding.

Every team manager needs to brief each one about their team and its mission statement. One of the most powerful ways of facilitating this sub-phase successfully is to hold a kickoff meeting. He needs to decide upon the most effective agenda for the meeting in terms of team member introduction, team rationale, ground rules, mission statement, guidelines, roles and management expectations. A time slot for open discussion is also a good way of addressing the confusion and the baseless guesses.

A team manager also needs to be aware of any inert cliques that may be underway. He must be vigilant to recognize the productive and counter-productive alliances. He needs to ensure that team members understand that their team is a collective project and explain the rationale behind inclusion of team members. A team manager, who accepts a team player attitude willingly, in a way, makes his role and leadership style as transparent as possible. This in turn, encourages team members to behave in a transparent fashion, and enables them to approach their team manager without any hesitation.

An ice breaker session is a very useful way of encouraging people to speak about themselves. This also lets the manager to get a fair idea of the kind of attitudes and skills that he has to deal with. It formulates appropriate training strategies for the future phases of team growth.

Certain elements like ground rules and standard operating procedures can be difficult to cover in one meeting. In such a case, every team manager needs to be directive enough to arrange for a 1-2 days of re-orientation training. Through this training, he can not only give a detailed overview about the ground rules and norms, but also address any concerns that his team members have. This in turn, guides him as well as team members to decide the course of action for the further phases of team development.

4.1.3 Growth Through Conflict—'Resetting Ground Rules for Solving Clashes'

This sub-phase is the most crucial of all the phases. This is the time when a team begins to realize the actual gravity of impending problems. They experience their first jitters of problems at various levels—interpersonal, technical, and with the management. The initial gusto is lessened, due to work pressures and control struggles. Anger and frustration begin to replace enthusiasm. Anger and frustration are sure-shot signs of negative conflict.

Another reason for having this sub-phase is that individual team members seem to have understood the roles and goals in the previous sub-phase, but when they come to this sub-phase, they tend to develop their own interpretations of the goals and roles. This individual interpretations lead to conflict of interests. A team manager needs to come to the fore to ensure that these conflicts are resolved or else they are bound to lead to the formation of different factions within a team.

Each one is trying to control the other. Each one is trying to encroach upon the other's functional boundary and this dissension leads to utter chaos, which in turn leads to the compromise of the mission. These clashes generate a slew of questions in the mind of each team member:

A. Am I a part of the right team?
B. Are the management expectations fair?
C. Does he (another team member) deserve this role?
D. Who should I support and which subgroups should I join?
E. Do I need to garner support by forming my own subgroup?
F. Are the mission and the formation of this team justifiable?

Every team manager needs to step in to reorient his team anchorages, and ensure that the above questions are answered on a first priority basis to resolve all misunderstandings and ego clashes within a team. Conflict is certainly acceptable and required, only when it is healthy and facilitative.

Depending upon the type of personalities and the complexity of the conflicts, this sub-phase can take up anywhere from weeks to months. This much amount of time is needed to ensure that teams forget about everything else and only concentrate on delivering performance-oriented results.

4.1.4 How to Facilitate Sub-phase 2

Many teams don't survive this sub-phase. This is the most crucial phase, their team manager in unison with team members has to work towards solving the interpersonal problems, plus has to keep reminding team members that they have the potential to perform and no one is weak or unfit.

Dynamic leadership is critical for this sub-phase. Proper training and support facilities need to be instituted in order to alter negative clashes into an environment of healthy conflict. It is important to conduct a revamp meeting, where the cloud of suspicion and doubt is cleared by reinforcing the mission statement, the rationale and the role of a team. At times, expectations and ground rules may have to be reset, to make everyone understand that each team member is equally important.

One of the most effective ways that can help everyone to reach compliance and a common level of agreement is to revisit the minutes of the kickoff meeting. The earlier this recap occurs, the lesser are the chances of misunderstandings and disagreements. It is a necessity for all team managers to lead by example. By showing tolerance and patience towards the new team, they are able to succeed in instilling patience amongst team members.

At times, team members have a problem with their immediate team manager/leader. They feel that their team manager is not accommodative enough and this results in frustration from their team manager's end. Instead of getting frustrated, a team manager needs to convince his team that he is not there to control them, but rather to facilitate the smooth functioning of a team. He needs to give an empathetic listening to all team concerns and issues, only then he will be able to convince them that he is on their side.

Each team manager needs to get things out in the open to eliminate hidden agendas and cross-purposes. He is supposed to act like a healing agent, whose aim is to get everyone together and forge a mutually satisfying reconciliation so as to strike out all that is unnecessary and detrimental to a team. Even a one-one session with problem team members is useful to sort things out rather than mudslinging in the open discussion. But he has to ensure that these one-one sessions do not generate undercurrents of politics. He needs to clearly state the purpose of these sessions to all team members. Here, he can also cite the examples of earlier teams, their positive experiences and success stories in order to encourage the current team to replicate the same success.

Regular orientation and counseling sessions foster positive conflict, which in turn leads to innovative ideas, skill development, and ensures smooth transition to the next phase. Also preparing for ensuing conflicts aids the transition to the next level.

4.2 Action Phase—'Managed Result-Driven Processes and Value Addition'

In this sub-phase, the team processes become more managed and start bringing about results which add value; there is more work and less talk. Team members by now are quite familiar with each other's working styles and personality traits. They have also learned ways of coping with personality clashes; rather they know how to leverage the various team member types. They have also fine tuned processes and ground rules are well outlined, well structured and better monitored. Team members function at a reasonably competent level. The team member types are well aligned to each other, and this lets team members act in a predictable and disciplined manner.

The action phase consists of two sub-phases:

A. Growth through acceptance

B. Growth through contribution

4.2.1 Growth Through Acceptance—'Setting Rules for Trust and Solidarity Building'

By the time a team reaches this sub-phase, they have realized the importance of healthy conflict, and have learned their lessons of what happens in an atmosphere of distrust and suspicion. They are in no mood to commit the same mistakes. Suspicion and distrust are replaced by acceptance. In this sub-phase, a team concentrates on ways of working through problems in unison. This is the sub-phase where the first of a positive team interaction is witnessed. It is during this sub-phase that new ground rules are identified and established, which could have been missed in the initial phases, these new ground rules ensure smooth decision-making. Every team member has a spool of the following set of questions spinning in his head:

A. What more can I do to contribute to the team?

B. What else can be done to solve the issues in a more amicable way?

C. What activities can we take up to improve the trust levels?

D. How can the team develop interpersonal skills?

E. What can be done to supersede the other teams?

F. What is the exact relationship between each team member, between each team member and his team manager?

G. What norms need to be formulated/reshaped to guide team behavior and interaction?

Here, a team specifies its own norms of acceptable team behavior, communication and conflict resolution. A team manager has to step in occasionally to review his team and its performance, but he has to make certain that he does not intervene in the day-to-day activities, as his team has installed ways of coping and co-surviving in a healthy way. By now team members have also worked out successful tools and methods of working.

They are in a better position to perform independently yet interdepend on each other in a beneficial way. They begin to perform with competence and also improve on their interpersonal skills. All this can be ensured with a team manager taking on a minimalist role.

The duration of this sub-phase is longer than the earlier two, as there are so many types of personalities and attitudes involved that need to be accommodated into the fabric of a team. Establishing trust does take time and maintaining it takes even longer.

4.2.2 How to Facilitate Sub-phase 3

Constant interaction and status updates—this is an ongoing process throughout this sub-phase. This assists team members to organize their own norms. Each team needs to constantly work together on developing ground rules, and encourage each other to accept and accede to these rules of operating procedures.

Timely feedback and review from their team manager plus objective peer-feedback, encourages team members to stay on track, and reinforce the clarity of their tasks and goals.

Another important aspect of team building in this sub-phase is working together in harmony when it comes to problem-solving. The earlier interference in each other's domain areas needs to be replaced with cooperation, and this can happen only when team members brainstorm and come up with innovative solutions for the technical problems that they face. This in turn, ensures that they are no more involved in control struggles, as they have come to realize that working in isolation works no wonders.

Team members need to be encouraged by letting them take on extra responsibilities in order to move a team to the next sub-phase. They need to involve themselves in a whole lot of cross-training activities, and also seek training in their own domain areas to achieve the next level of efficiency.

A team manager is constantly required to reinforce the ground rules by encouraging team members to adopt professionalism while conducting themselves in a team. He needs to ensure that his team receives regular doses of motivation, and finds out ways of encouraging team members to respect each other's personalities and skill-set. He also needs to work out strategies for honing individual skills in respect to team goals.

By the end of this sub-phase, team members trust each other and there is very little scope for dissension. They learn to give space to each other and no one acts or reacts in isolation. They have been able to overcome their personal differences, and by now they are in a position to perform with full competence and that too in collaboration.

4.2.3 Growth Through Contribution—'Getting the Act Together'

By the time team members reach this sub-phase, their team has 'been there and done that'. By now they have formulated time tested methods of executing their work effectively. They know how to draw out a roadmap and stick to it.

In this sub-phase, team members are at their peak performance level and goals are achieved within the given constraints. Team performs to produce the desired outcome through effective and efficient working practices, and there is a synergy of individual contributions. The trust earned in the previous sub-phases is strengthened by another important aspect, which is the 'pride' team members take in team success and achievements. Each team member takes pride in being a part of a highly cohesive team. Team members are aware of the strengths and weaknesses of each team member. Strengths are appreciated and everyone works in unison towards overcoming the weaknesses of each other.

Here, most of the questions posed in the earlier phases have found their solutions, which translate into various advantages like:

A. Satisfied team members and team managers.

B. Satisfied top management.

C. Productivity is at its peak. Along with team progress, personal growth is also encouraged.

D. Team members are highly enthusiastic about their roles.

E. Proactive attitude towards problems and conflicts, thereby reducing the impact of risks.

F. At times, they take lucrative decisions even without being steered by inputs from the management executive.

G. Positive interpersonal relationships are effectuated. Everyone knows the ground rules of interacting with the various roles that are present in a team, thereby ensuring hassle-free communication channels.

H. Loyalty towards the team. There are no hidden agendas as everyone is working towards one common goal. The 'I-attitude' is replaced with group-thinking, 'We-attitude.'

4.2.4 How to Facilitate Sub-phase 4

In this phase, a team does not need much of facilitation, either from within or directional support from its team manager. Even if a team is very much self-directed, regular sessions of keeping the enthusiasm level high are always needed. Motivation in the form of appreciation needs to be given by its team manager on a timely basis.

Another important aspect for ensuring the success of this sub-phase is to give equal opportunity to all. It is necessary for a team manager to adopt several techniques like assigning higher roles to team members or role-rotation. These methods ensure that everyone is equally valued and organizations have full faith in each of their resources. This not only increases loyalty towards team managers but also towards organizations, thereby preserving the organizational culture of honesty and fairness. Over management in this phase is not good at all. Team members are willing to accept more responsibility, only if management isn't constantly looking over their shoulder.

Rewarding a team's performance is as important as recording a team's performance. Performance management and performance measurement are key contributors to improved team management. Goals have to be measurable and specific. Creating score cards is an efficacious way of improving performance. The policy of reward and recognition strengthens a team as an efficient unit. This in turn results in laser sharp focus on following through the team charter.

Every team manager has to remember that this sub-phase is all about empowering team members and role sharing.

4.3 Results Phase—'Self-direction and Organization Level Maturity'

Teams not only become self-sustaining mature units, but also translate their success at the organizational level in terms of quality improvement and process maturity. The team processes, interactions and results are more stabilized and agile. Team members are better equipped to face challenges in the proactive mode. All the elements of a team operate in a synthesized manner. The repeated cycle of performance fosters a culture of excellence in every organization.

The results phase consists of two sub-phases:

A. Growth through repeated success

B. Growth through networking

4.3.1 Growth Through Repeated Success—'Going One Step Beyond'

This sub-phase takes the team development process to a new level of process maturity. This process goes one step beyond the previous four phases. It demonstrates that team development is not simply about achieving the goals and then forgetting about the very nucleus that achieved those goals.

Here, there could be two routes to this sub-phase: (a) team has achieved the desired mission, or (b) team has completed an important milestone and moves to the next level of the roadmap.

This sub-phase is all about making team members feel valued by their organization. It is about making team members realize that they have enriched themselves by being a part of a dynamic venture. Even while exiting from a team, they experience a myriad of emotions:

A. Sense of loss that the team is going to dissolve.

B. Sense of achievement as the desired goal has been realized.

C. Sense of instability as to what is going to be the next assignment.

4.3.2 How to Facilitate Sub-phase 5

The most important method of facilitating this sub-phase is celebrating and recognizing team achievements. A team manager needs to hold a round up/project end meeting, where every team member is given his due recognition.

Apart from this, it is also advantageous for a team to assign time towards the discussion of what went well and what could have been avoided. All these findings can be recorded in a lessons learned document. This document is advantageous to team members in their future roles and also acts as a knowledge repository for existing teams.

A team manager is also required to be sensitive to the emotional state of instability that team members are experiencing. He needs to comfort his team members, by telling them that they are going to find a new place soon in a new team, and he also needs to assure them that this forthcoming experience is going to be as rewarding as the current one. He also needs to express his personal as well as organization's gratitude for team contributions and success.

4.3.3 Growth Through Networking—'Best Practices, Supportive Strategies'

Each self-managed team develops its own best practices, which contribute to achieving their goal, and can serve as strategies useful for other teams and the entire organization.

By the time teams reach this stage, the roles have reversed, all this while they were the ones needing facilitation support, but now their performance-oriented nature makes organizations more responsive and adaptable to today's rapidly changing world.

All this while, teams needed to be oriented and adapted to environments where they would be able to work in a comfortable manner, now, it is their chance to provide a kind of environment for organizations to move to the next level of performance.

4.3.4 How to Facilitate Sub-phase 6

One of the most effective ways of facilitating this sub-phase is by assigning specialized tasks, where team members need to step out of their functional boundaries and mingle with other units to become experts. In the process, they get an opportunity to transform the organizational level processes and policies positively, and at the same time they too bring back something substantial and positive to their team.

Intrinsic value is the key to ensuring that this network of self-directed work teams survives. Each organization needs to constantly institute innovative ways of empowering staff and encouraging professional development to create that feeling of intrinsic value.

What is the one most important factor that keeps this entire process going, did I hear corporate directive… theoretically speaking that is the correct answer, but practically 'Selfless Cooperation and Self-Initiative' works wonders.

4.4 More Facilitation Tips—'Applicable to All Phases'

1. A team manager in order to strengthen the foundations of a self-directed work team must keep these points in mind:
   - I. He is a collaborative colleague, not the final authority.
   - II. He leads by example, not by giving out orders.
   - III. He is a facilitator, not the final decision-maker.
2. Regularly discuss the team growth process and review the team characteristics of each sub-phase in order to design corrective measures.
3. Motivate team members to self-monitor their behavioral patterns in various team-related processes like communication, meetings, feedback, etc.
4. Don't "fix" the team problems, have each team work out solutions.

5. At times, a team manager may need the services of an outside coach to guide him in providing a team with clear role definitions.
6. Focus on constructive ways of organizing the work.
7. Teams need to be oriented and adapted to environments so that they can comfortably work with other levels in an organization.
8. Teams must be encouraged to use more advanced problem solving techniques.

4.5 A Pictorial Recap—'The Six Phases of Team Growth'

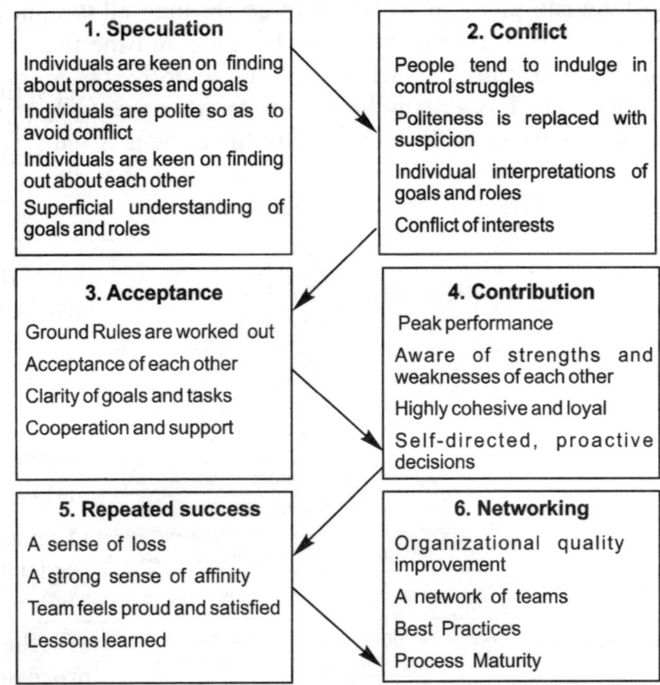

Fig. 4.1: The Six Phases of Team Growth

4.6 The Advantage Pyramid—'Evolve a Star Team'

The advantage pyramid of the 'OAR' phases of development of an SDWT is depicted as follows, and which I have already explained in the preceding paragraphs. As time goes by, a team becomes fully operational and begins to give its best, and the advantages only multiply.

This entire cycle of maturity is *recursive* and *interrelated*. For example, if in a particular team the number of personalities is more, then it is likely that a team loops forth and back between the sub-phase 1 and sub-phase 2 more than once in order to set things in order. Another example of cycling through the phases more than once in the life of a team is when it has completed all six phases, and then to rectify certain conditions which the concerned team discovers after either the growth through repeated performance or growth through networking sub-phase, it will have to go through all the phases once more. The difference between this time and the first time is that the transition is much faster and smoother as most of the groundwork has already been laid. Another scenario where a team may have to undergo the entire life cycle is when a new team member joins in, as it is quite possible that he could challenge the current norms and ground rules.

Fig. 4.2: The Advantage Pyramid

No matter what, each team has to go through all of the above phases, whether a team is a result of a new experiment that an organization has taken up or it is a new component of a well established administrative setup. The above diagram is representative of the figure titled 'The Nucleus of Benefits'.

Now you know why a team needs to go through all of those phases. Only after it reaches its fruition right from Speculation-> Conflict-> Acceptance-> Contribution->Repeated Success->Networking, will each organization be able to reap the gamut of benefits shown in the 'The Advantage Pyramid' diagram. As you can notice that the segment of the last sub-phase is larger than the first one, this is indicative of the fact that the number of advantages increases as one rows further in the team maturity cycle, i.e., from O to R, from sub-phase 1 towards sub-phase 6.

4.7 Worksheet for Team Growth

Team Growth Evaluation

The Team Growth Evaluation worksheet helps a team and its team manager to identify the phase in which the SDWT is, and what aspects need to be worked on, in order to move to the next phase. This worksheet is normally filled up by team manager based on his observations and team inputs.

Team Name:

Note: You can either rate on the basis of 1 (lowest) to 6 (highest) and/or include observations in the columns

Behavior, Function	Sub-Phase 1	Sub-Phase 2	Sub-Phase 3	Sub-Phase 4	Sub-Phase 5	Sub-Phase 6
Keenness Level						
Conflict of Interests						
Control Struggles						
Well Planned Ground Rules						
Team Identity						
Acceptance Level						
Responsibility						
Goal Clarity						

(Contd...)

Cooperation						
Work Style						
Agility						
Trust						
Sense of Affinity						
Process Maturity						
Networking						
Sense of Pride						
Quality Enhancement						

Team manager's additional observations:

Specific team behavioral dynamics:

Measures to be taken:

Place a tick against those statements that are valid:

1. The team is trying to create its identity.
2. The team has established its identity and knows how to maintain it.
3. There is conflict in the team as it is trying to find out individual members' goals and roles.
4. Team members share a common vision.
5. Team members do not yet know what to expect of each other and hence fail to deliver.
6. There is consistency in performance.
7. There is a great deal of personality clashes.
8. Team members are supporting each other and work well with each other.
9. Team members are intolerant of the diversity.
10. The team has learned the techniques of leveraging the diverse skills of its team members.
11. Team members are more interested in their own accomplishments as they are still trying to create a rightful place for themselves.
12. The team as an integrated unit celebrates accomplishments.
13. Doubt the validity of the team's purpose and goals.
14. Strong sense of belief in the team goals.
15. Place the blame for failure on other team members.
16. Constructive conflicts are present.

(Contd...)

17.	Lack of individual contribution.
18.	Individual contribution, individual growth and eventually team growth.
19.	Blaming the organization for lack of support and hence poor results.
20.	Real results.

4.8 Benchmarks for Successful Team Development

The characteristics stated as follows are a sure shot confirmation that a team has matured well, by going through all the phases successfully:

1. Each team member is highly overenthusiastic about his role and about cooperating with the rest towards the goal fulfillment process.
2. Team members indulge in objective and beneficial assessment of each other.
3. A climate of trust and mutual cooperation exists in a team. There is no room for the grapevine, subgroups, suspicion or negative agendas.
4. There is a high level of interdependence amongst team members.
5. Dynamic and facilitative leadership is in place.
6. Team members are absolutely clear on their tasks, roles and the dependency links amongst themselves.
7. A team is willing to take risks and decisions in order to adhere to the team mission.
8. A team strictly follows standard operating practices regarding communication, negotiation, conflict resolution, escalation and assessment.
9. Each team member knows what the target is and what has to be done in order to achieve the same.
10. Team members take pride and satisfaction, both in individual and team success.
11. Team members are willing to step out of the comfort zone by implementing innovative ideas.
12. Team members have a strong sense of affinity towards their team.

4.9 Chapter Recap

1. A team has different needs at different times, and this is where the OAR model of team growth comes into picture.
2. In the organizing phase, a team is struggling to find an identity through speculation and conflict. In the action phase, it is striving hard through acceptance and collaboration to maintain its identity and vision. In the results phase, each team is impacting not only itself, but also its organization through its repeated performance and networking abilities.
3. The Advantage Pyramid exemplifies the fact that the number of advantages keeps on increasing, as a team evolves through the initial phases of anticipation till the final stages of stability and self-initiation.

PART II

From Thinking to Action: Bringing About the Transformation

5

The Four Facets Model of Team Management—'The Core Components'

The four facets of team management help employees to go from a non-committed group to a highly focused team. The right techniques for building an energy-driven team, based on a collective sense of accountability, bring about the desired results. Let me give you an analogy for these four facets. The base of an organization can be likened to the foundation of a building. Just as slabs of concrete strengthen the foundation of a building, in the same light SDWTs strengthen the base of an organization. Just as a wheel's weight bearing capacity depends upon the strength of its hub, similarly the strength of a team has a strong influence on the performance of an organization. Thus, the *hub* of any organization is its *teams*.

5.1 The Four Facets Flow—'Drive Powerfully Ahead'

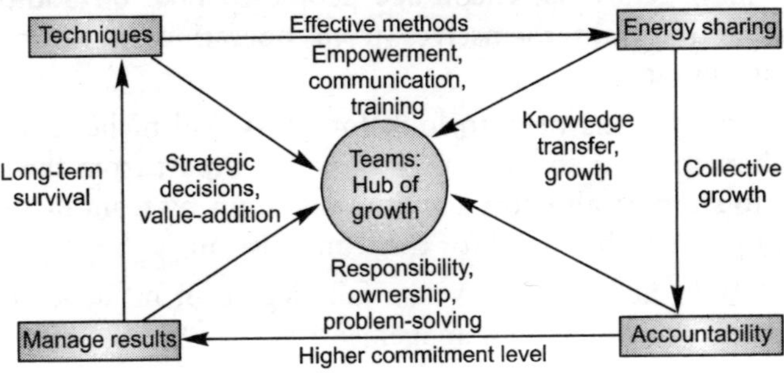

Fig. 5.1: The Four Facets Flow Diagram

The above flow is elucidated in the subsequent sections.

5.2 Techniques of Team Management—'Co-share Corporate Success'

Inherent creativity needs to be tapped,
Only then benefits derived will be apt.

The team management techniques work at four levels:

First level is to energize teams and reduce friction.

Second level is about helping team members understand and relate to each other's needs and preferences.

Third level is about knowledge enhancement and skill development.

All the above levels build the base on which the fourth level is built, this level corresponds to building and sustaining of a new work culture.

5.2.1 Empowerment—'Broaden the Scope of Employee Involvement'

Empowering team members is the key technique to developing high performance teams. Empowering facilitates them to develop the sense of ownership necessary to accomplish the team's charter. Empowering does not mean mere delegation, but rather it is entrusting a team with higher level responsibilities. It's about creating decision-makers.

Employee empowerment and the diversity that comes with it, is an absolute essential for continuous improvement. Organizations need to design plans and strategies to increase opportunities for self-initiated management. In addition to this, team managers must encourage people to take on additional roles, and refrain themselves from operating in the micro-manage mode.

Organizations need to look for cross-skill niches for team members in order to strengthen their CV. Apart from this; they need to support all extra activities taken up by team members, which prove to be useful for the team mission.

SDWTs need to be given a fair degree of influence in the various aspects of team management:

- Provide inputs for shaping the vision.
- Combined results will only work when team members have influence over each other.
- Be able to contribute to budget and deadline decisions.
- They need to have the choice to select new team members and remove underperformers.

Empowerment is the key to everlasting collaborations. The success of this factor rests on the **SAR** triangle of balance—sense of ownership, accountability and responsibility. Keeping this balance in sight is a major prerequisite while assembling any new team.

5.2.2 Communication—'Share Ideas, Listen Well, Perform Better'

Clarity of purpose and tasks begins with smooth communication. A team manager needs to ensure that the vision statement from the higher-ups reaches his team in the most definite and clear manner, as it is this vision, which is the strongest factor that brings people together.

If team members are controlled unnecessarily and feel restrained, then not only do they feel undervalued, but also upset that they are not allowed to express and discuss their hopes and problems. Regular communication in the form of formal team meetings or informal impromptu sessions, encourages exchange of feedback, ideas, concerns and solutions.

Too often, some of the team members or even their team manager is too rash to discount people's inputs and ideas, because they have their own ideas and want to hog all the limelight by implementing their ideas. This is the most disastrous form of behavior because of which many intelligent ideas go down the drain. There need to be clear guidelines about communication equality and they need to be strictly performed so as to allow everyone to participate in the decision-making process.

'Open door' policy is essential to encourage everyone to raise their opinions and issues. Each team manager needs to find team members who have not spoken during the team interaction sessions and encourage them to interact. Top executives too, have to encourage communication from team members because this is how they can get lucrative suggestions, which many a time become the driving force for new organizational practices.

5.2.3 Training—'Critical to Success'

The management needs to devote time and efforts for developing training programs. The programs need to be designed in such a way that the skills and potential of each and every resource are enhanced. Training must occupy an important place in the corporate agenda.

In order to train the employees correctly, an organization at times may have to hire external trainers, or may have to better the standard of teaching of their own internal trainers.

Team members in conjunction with their team manager, need to devote quality time for drawing the career path and a solid plan to realize it. Team managers need to actually sit down with employees to work out learning objectives—their job just does not stop here, they need to go beyond this. They need to keep a tab on the progress of every potential employee, review the learning curve, and design an action plan to correct discrepancies. Seeking inputs from team members on performance levels is also a good way of ensuring that a team continues to be a self-initiated collective effort as not only their performance but also their inputs for improving performance are valued.

At the organizational level, the training courses and their contents have to be reviewed periodically, and their results have to be compared with the productivity rates of the employees. Review and revision of training programs, development courses and refresher courses on a timely basis is important for keeping pace with competition, both internal as well as external.

5.2.4 Crystal Clear Understanding—'Unified Team Culture'

It is essential for an SDWT and its facilitating team manager to draft a team charter or team agreement, whereby a team knows what exactly is expected from it. These expectations can be applied to a gamut of team activities, right from formal team meetings to coffee break discussions. The charter is a set of comprehensive terms by which a team is going to operate, and this enables each team member to be on the same page of understanding and makes him feels at par with others.

Following the charter leads to clear understanding of what has to be done and how it has to be done. The charter leads to a *transparent* way of functioning. Team members behave in an objective manner and the processes are executed well. Team managers and the top management have to ensure that there is 100 per cent buy-in from team members before finalizing and implementing the charter. Constant check has to be kept on the values and behaviors demonstrated by team members while operating in a team. Corrective feedback and punishment is something that a team manager is required to handle diligently.

As there is collective buy-in from the entire team and everyone is held equally responsible, team members tend to act in a coordinated manner to preserve the team values. Over the course of time, they themselves become capable of counter checking discrepant team behaviors. The values and behaviors a team subscribes to are of utmost importance for smoothing out the functioning of a team. A team becomes dysfunctional in times of pressure, if these are not precisely stated and adhered to. It is a prerequisite for the team charter to have comprehensive provisions for the same, which aids the understanding process of team members. It enables them to clearly know what is expected from them in terms of behaviors needed to live by the values.

Another important aspect that can be reinforced is the mission statement. Encapsulating the objectives of the mission in the charter, keeps team members focused and brings them together. This charter keeps the gusto going by ensuring that a team has high understanding of all the processes, challenges, advantages, dependencies, targets, values and their roles.

5.2.5 Conflict Management—'Capitalize on Personality Diversity'

Barriers in communication channels are among the most important factors that lead to conflicts. The points discussed under the communication head convert a combative climate to a collaborative one. A conflict resolution strategy has four levels to it, which are:

Informal: Where teams discuss the problem and try to self-correct the same.

Mediator: In case the informal meeting does not come to any solution, then a team manager needs to mediate between the conflicting parties.

Formal discussion: Even after mediation, if the problem is not settled, then a team needs to openly discuss the issue without indulging in finger pointing.

Escalation: The last resort is escalation where the conflict needs to be handled by a senior executive depending on the escalation points decided in the escalation policy.

All the above techniques reflect one thing—discussion and not discord. Positive conflict is about healthy competition and healthy discussion, while negative conflict is about confrontation. In either case, the above points come in handy to resolve the situation. The following are the modes of conflict resolution but the best one is that of cooperation, as it upholds the spirit of collaboration, gives equal credit to all and provides long lasting resolutions. The rest of the modes can be implemented in certain cases where the importance of the problem at hand is low or not urgent.

1. **Avoidance**: This mode is about withdrawal. No one is willing to come forward to discuss and solve the conflict. This leaves a team high and dry.
2. **Accommodative**: It is about accepting others' viewpoint without asserting yourself. It's purely based on a high level of cooperation. Do not confuse this

with the cooperative/collaborative mode. In the accommodative mode, there is not much discussion or exchange of views.

3. **Competition:** Often the decision is more favorable to the party who has more influence over the conflict resolution process. This means that the source of dissatisfaction is uprooted only temporarily and is likely to resurface with more gravity, sometime soon.
4. **Compromise:** Here the involved stakeholders meet together to discuss the conflict and resolve their differences by negotiation. They reach an agreement by consensus. It's a give and take policy, which leads to the compromise of the team mission.
5. **Cooperation:** Here people are willing to cooperate not only for analyzing the issue, but also for coming up with a positive solution. It is about assertiveness and collaboration.

5.2.6 Mentoring—'Changing Times, Changing Roles'

Mentoring and tutoring sessions are essential not only for addressing team problems but also interpersonal stakes. A team manager needs to indulge in motivating continued contributions on a continual basis. Counseling lets a team manager to capture both positive and negative feedback from a team about various aspects, including his own style of leadership, which assists in solving critical hitches.

Team managers are required to constantly update their mentoring skills in order to deal with extremes of team problems, right from team meetings to introvert team members. One of the most important skills that a team manager is required to possess is that of empathetic listening. A team manager also needs to induct team members in the most efficient way. For example, if a new team member joins a fully functioning SDWT, then his team manager needs to have a one-to-one session with the new entrant to explain to him about the team goals and the various expectations. He then needs to introduce the new team member to the rest of a team. It is always beneficial for a team manager to keep in touch with a new team member on a constant basis for the initial few weeks until he feels settled down. Team managers can also appoint another team member to facilitate the new member's induction through the buddy system policy.

From the regular mentoring meetings, team managers are able to get a feel of individual motivational needs and design appropriate methods for motivating team members. From a personal one-on-one meeting, team managers are also able to gauge the motivation level of the coachee from the voice tone, body language and other non-verbal cues.

To ensure that each team member is able to exert a fair degree of influence, a team manager ought to be an excellent facilitator. Even during team meetings, a team manager needs to ensure that there is no lopsided communication—everyone is entitled to equal airtime. Giving equal airtime does not mean that a team manager has to agree to all the concerns, rather he must use his vigilance to guide his team to productive outcomes, by ensuring that only genuine concerns are taken care of.

All team managers need to make efforts to fully explore the options of enabling teams to achieve their dreams. Regular reality checks and feedback help team managers to classify problem areas. Discussion with team members aids a team manager to design various options for achieving the goals. Mentoring is about encouraging team members without manipulating their goals. It is always wise that team managers follow up agreements on a one-to-one basis.

Mentoring and coaching have to be on every team manager's agenda.

5.2.7 Example—'New Kid on the Block'

Problem Statement

Bran, a new recruit joined a sales team which had been functioning since the past six months. All team members were well trained in all aspects of team management and were a close knit group. Bran was extremely nervous even after two months, as he still felt out of place and derived no job satisfaction at all. He approached his team manager to work out a solution. "Rick, I feel out of place. May be we could have a formal introduction session, where I can get to know the team and *vice versa*. Also we need to have a one-one session, where you can tell me about my exact role, processes and values." "I don't think all this is necessary, as you have a sales background of four years, you ought to be able to deliver," retorted Rick.

His team manager was really not willing to put up with Bran's nervousness and did not want to discuss about it at all. Bran's team manager strongly felt that the one day induction session was good enough to get Bran started. With this non-cooperative attitude of both team members and his team manager, Bran felt absolutely isolated. Though he has much to contribute, he does not do so, as his team members and team manager simply ignored and treated him as an unwanted junior.

Problem Analysis

A new member feels isolated, if he is not given the right kind of training, support and encouragement. The non-cooperation movement against Bran was the main reason for both his frustration and non-performance.

This isolation could have been avoided, if the team manager had informed the team about Bran and his role. It's both the team and team manager's job to introduce and involve a new member in the team. At the same time, the new member must be made familiar with procedures, processes and interfaces of his new assignment.

Solution

A team as a whole is responsible for the successful induction of a new entrant. Every team manager along with the rest of his team needs to provide adequate integration in terms of knowledge transfer, buddy system, mentoring and training. These factors are more important in the early phases of new induction.

A team manager has to be easily accessible and approachable to his team members and their grievances, especially in the case of new entrants. He needs to have an orientation system in place that continues up to a reasonable period of time after a new employee joins in, to ensure that the integration and adjustment are happening in a healthy way.

An SDWT is the extended family of team members, therefore, it is essential to match the personality of a new member with that of his team and organization. He needs to be encouraged and trained to imbibe the values and beliefs of his team and organization. Both, team members and their team manager, need to indulge in a series of candid discussions with the new member on what is his role, his expectations, team values, processes and support structures. This kind of constant interaction facilitates smooth induction.

A team must support and induct a new member by sharing guidelines, practices, and handbooks. Team members cooperate with the new member, only when their team manager encourages them to do so. Orientation and training is a major responsibility that both old team members and team manager are required to fulfill in order to avoid any kind of alienation.

5.2.8 Advantages of the Above Techniques

A. Involving teams in creating direction through empowerment generates commitment. The freedom to choose leads to the feeling of being valued.

B. Hassle free communication aids in the process of understanding and being understood. High level of understanding ensures that team members know exactly where they are going and how fast they are going to get there. They are aware of all the functional dependencies and challenges involved, thereby making them proactive in approach.

C. Minimize escalation of conflict.

D. The strengths of various personalities are leveraged.

E. Internal communications can also be improved by involving senior staff whenever possible. Regular team meetings also allow communication to flow more freely and encourage an exchange of ideas.

5.3 Energy Sharing—'Create Phenomenal Momentum'

Energy is the most valuable intangible asset
Of an organization,
Which sets positive change
In motion.

Energy sharing is all about collaborative leadership. Each team member is a leader in his own way as he comes with a unique baggage of skills, personality and myriad team experiences.

Energy sharing enables the SDWTs to not only achieve the mission, but also successfully set performance goals and develop robust strategies to manage change. A positive support system in terms of counseling, mentoring, rewards, broader assignments and recognition is the key to energy multiplication.

In the process of identifying star potential, do not introduce unnecessary competition; rather look for ways in which knowledge energy can be shared by identifying the skills. Apart from building positive vibes in the professional setup, a team needs to have off-site team activities in order to foster cooperation and trust.

How do you eliminate negative energy or non-performing energy? —>Team members need to know their roles and expectations clearly. In spite of clear definition, if they still do not give their best then merely removing them from a team won't solve the problem. Along with their team manager, the concerned team members need to discuss the gaps, and document the findings and observations on problematic behavior.

It can so happen that the concerned team member has been assigned a role not befitting his skills and that is why he is not able to contribute. Another example is that he has been trained for the assigned role, but due to some internal structural changes, he is assigned to a different role altogether. In such cases, alternatives need to be worked out. This is where empowerment and cross-training come in handy.

In case of team members who act conversely to team culture and their actions are against team values, such team members need to be dealt with on the highest priority level. A team manager in consultation with the rest of his team needs to act quickly to get these toxic team members off board. Self-managed teams are vigilant enough to pinpoint negative performers, depending on the performance benchmarks and their feedback, a team manager can marginalize the underperformers and finally remove them. Toxic, non-cooperative resources are the biggest threat to a team manager's status and team morale.

It is not about energy sharing within team limits only; it is about energy vibes flowing from the management towards a team too. The management needs to ensure that each team believes that it's not just about organizational growth, but also about collective progress.

5.3.1 Example—'The Star-crossed Performer'

Problem Statement

Rick, a junior system analyst was furious at what just transpired in the weekly status update meeting. He walked over to his friend's desk to vent out his humiliation. "This is not fair. I too was an integral part of the purchase flow module, but the senior system analyst reported it entirely under his name. The purchase flow was a joint effort. I too added my intelligent energy to its development." "Calm down and tell me what happened exactly," inquired his friend Shaun. "We just had our weekly status update session, and you won't believe my entire work for the last week was attributed to the efforts of the senior business analyst," responded Rick.

His friend advised him to have a word with his immediate senior, the senior system analyst. "I did so, but no use. He said it really doesn't matter under whose name the work is reported as long as it is completed. According to him, I am overreacting. The team manager also did not set things straight for me," replied Rick in a dejected tone.

Problem Analysis

The main cause of worry is that the concerned team manager simply assigns duties, and does not keep a vigilant watch on the reporting and energy sharing patterns. Even when a team member informs him of a faulty pattern, he chooses to ignore it, thereby disrupting the flow of positive energy sharing. This discourages Rick from contributing his knowledge and expertise in future.

Any negative trend including false reporting of work, tends to create a climate of unhealthy vibes and compromises the norms that govern fair team behavior. The careless attitude of the senior system analyst is a big source of friction, put downs and ill feelings.

Solution

A team manager's duty does not end with mere role assignments, rather it is his duty to monitor team assignments on a regular basis, and ensure that all provisions are in place to fuel positive energy sharing. Listening, hearing, and acknowledging team member updates and complaints is a critical function of any team manager, as these three aspects go to show that he values each team member's energy inputs equally and won't tolerate any faulty behavior.

There needs to be a system of checks and counterchecks in place to handle problem employees, by first counseling them, then reprimanding them, then marginalizing them and finally taking tough decisions of transfer or termination, to preserve the fabric of a team. Both, a team and its team manager, need to be adept at developing a common language for openly discussing differences in how team members use their energy, and how this diversity in perspective can bring about better results.

Energizing a team is everyone's duty. Although each team manager has to initiate energizing activities and behaviors, but maintaining high energy levels is the main responsibility of team members. When a team manager demonstrates his genuine respect for the energy shared in his team, only then team members follow in his footsteps, and respect each other and share sincere praise for their collective wisdom.

5.3.2 Worksheets for Energy Sharing

Collaboration Plan

The Collaboration Plan worksheet refines and prioritizes the actions needed to implement the proposed ideas, processes and tools in a collaborative mode. The worksheet is to be filled up by team managers with inputs from employees.

Collaboration Plan for the: Month/Quarter/Given Period: Key ideas, suggestions, and feedback: List of energy sharing areas from highest to lowest priority along with timetable and monitoring details:	
Areas of Energy Sharing	**Description Collaborating Team Members**
Communication	• Who will monitor and implement the processes and tools • Who will stick to which ground rules
Decision-making	• How inputs will be collected and shared
Status Updates	• Means and tools of sharing • Response time guidelines
Information Transfer	• Who will develop and deliver presentations • Who will conduct internal training
Team Growth	• Kind of opportunities, value creation team members offer each other
Quality of Knowledge Energy	• Is knowledge provided in an accessible place • Is it complete, relevant, timely and accurate • Who is responsible for these factors

Energy Building

The responses to the Energy Building worksheet aid a team manager and his team in determining team members that complement each other and add value to the team mission. At the same time, inputs from team members also help to discuss and develop methods of integrating 'problem' members into the high-participation work environment.

<table>
<tr><td colspan="4">Team Member Name:</td></tr>
<tr><td>Special skills, knowledge</td><td>History of energy sharing</td><td>Comfort level in conflict (specific examples)</td><td>Cooperation rating (specific examples)</td></tr>
<tr><td></td><td></td><td></td><td></td></tr>
<tr><td colspan="4">Inputs from the team member:
What are some of the energy sharing obstacles that the team is currently facing:
What would you do to address these obstacles:
State instances where strong energy sharing was present:
Prioritize goals for improved energy sharing:</td></tr>
</table>

<table>
<tr><td>Colleague name</td><td>Absolute compatibility</td><td>Moderate level of energy sharing</td><td>Always in conflict</td><td>Key observations</td></tr>
<tr><td></td><td></td><td></td><td></td><td></td></tr>
<tr><td colspan="5">Team manager's feedback and recommendations:</td></tr>
</table>

5.3.3 *Advantages of Energy Sharing*

A. There is continuous improvement.

B. 'Grow Together' is the sure fire *mantra* for the climate of co-existence.

C. Energy sharing is the source of competitive advantage. It is the base of a knowledge economy.

D. Team members and top management work in unison by deriving value from information energy shared amongst them.

5.4 Accountability—'Roll up Your Sleeves and Get Going'

Own up without fear
So that quantum progress occurs,
Year after year.

Accountability is all about ownership and responsibility. In team culture, it is focused on the entire team rather than the individual. The SDWT as a whole accepts responsibility for the consequences. In today's times, team accountability is bringing about a 'Responsibility Revolution'.

In high performance teams, mutual accountability is very crucial. Team accountability is about collectively fixing things when they go wrong. The main aspects that control the accountability facet are clear definition of the mission, and the roles and responsibilities. Accountable teams enforce a peer-to-peer accountability, where team members are so committed to the goals that they are constantly reminding each other when any team members go off track.

In order to hold people accountable, the management needs to ensure that they are given the required level of authority to perform the duties and steer the processes to produce the desired consequences. There is no point in holding someone accountable, if he is not given the authority to manage the business processes. The level of accountability depends on how clearly team goals have been stipulated. Establishing interdependence in a team's work also ensures collective sense of accountability.

Team members need to be given the privilege to influence other team member's behavior for positive reasons. An organization that fosters an environment of accountability, trains its teams to view mistakes and failures as learning opportunities rather than opportunities for blaming people. In the latter case, people tend to be secretive in nature and belittle the others to gain undue advantage in unfair competition. Organizations and team managers need to encourage team members to shift from finger pointing to constructive ways of solving accountability failures. It is necessary for them to make each team member realize that just as the fruits of success are enjoyed by the entire team, the same is applicable to the consequences of failure.

In the initial stages of the team building process, every team manager is responsible for steering the direction of team meetings. He has to make team members realize the importance of discussing action plans of what has to be done to reverse failure rather than to focus on what was done. He also needs to encourage team members to support each other to solve performance issues.

Again every organization has to apply the above tips at three levels of accountability—Personal accountability, accountability to the other team members and accountability to the outsiders. It is highly crucial that people truly understand responsibilities, performance metrics, constraints, and potential consequences in order to imbibe the value of accountability.

5.4.1 Example—'When Team Accountability is Just Talk'

Problem Statement

Jerry, a software architect was on leave for a week and all his tasks were assigned to his colleague Harris by their team manager. The team manager had been sending e-mails to Harris requesting certain figures, but there was no response from Harris, he simply ignored the mails.

After two days of incessant e-mailing, he called Harris for a discussion. "Harris I have been sending you e-mails on Jerry's account, but you did not bother to respond. Why?" "Well Sir, because responding to Jerry's mail is not part of my duty, I am not accountable for it," said Harris. "Obviously, it's your duty. You have taken over his assignments for this week. I also e-mailed you regarding this," reprimanded his team manager. "Yes Sir, but you never mentioned anything about e-mails and that's why I did not respond as I thought I am not responsible for answering e-mails," replied Harris defensively.

Problem Analysis

Both the team manager and Harris are at fault. The main reason for this accountability issue is the lack of constant and clear communication about task assignments. The take it for granted attitude of the team manager and the non-accountable adamancy of the team member leads to a flare up. Without relevant information from the team manager, Harris was not clear on the accountability aspect of Jerry's duties.

In mutually accountable teams, team members cooperate with each other without questioning each other. In this example team accountability is just talk. Had the team members really been accountable to the team, then Harris himself would have asked his team manager about the missing aspects while taking up Jerry's duties for a week, and would have performed the duties in all sincerity. Even the team manager would have led the team by example, by giving detailed instructions regarding accountability and wouldn't have waited for two whole days to go unproductive.

Solution

All non-accountable, non-performing actions of a team need to be directly dealt with. Every team manager must clarify exactly what needs to be achieved, who needs to deliver what, and how everyone is to behave in order to achieve the results. Assumptions are dangerous and have no place in team accountability.

With clear role definition in place, team members can never dare to tear a team manager down; instead they roll up their sleeves and get involved. When all are committed, shared leadership gets created. If things are going hay wire, a team manager needs to step in immediately to correct any disorientation. Proactive performance management is a priority one requirement for collective accountability.

Simple but effective things like a workshop, where team members learn different ways on how to improve accountability, works wonders. Regular meetings dedicated to addressing team problems are critical for unearthing accountability issues.

Harris would not have been able to shirk his responsibility, had his team manager discussed his new duties in detail and got his unconditional buy-in on the temporary assignment.

5.4.2 Worksheets for Accountability

Accountability Evaluation

The Accountability Evaluation worksheet identifies team players in terms of responsibility, ownership and accountability, both on an individual as well as collective basis. The rating column determines the future course of action in the case of faulty team member behavior.

<table>
<tr><td colspan="4">Name of the Team Member:
Modules/Tasks Responsible for:
Overall Level of Willingness to take up ownership:
What are the key issues:</td></tr>
<tr><td>Accountability Item</td><td>Description</td><td>Recommendation/ Action Plans</td><td>Ratings (Low 0-15, Medium 16-30, High 31-45)</td></tr>
<tr><td>Joint creation and realization of team goals</td><td>• Does he contribute a fair share of accountability to all team members
• How involved is he in the process of defining and achieving goals</td><td></td><td></td></tr>
<tr><td>Attitude towards team outcomes</td><td>• Does he share both success and failure equally
• In times of failure whether he puts in extra efforts to reverse failure into productive outcome</td><td></td><td></td></tr>
<tr><td>Opportunities for involvement</td><td>• Level of involvement exhibited</td><td></td><td></td></tr>
<tr><td>Traits of a team player</td><td>• Does he willingly take up ownership for areas outside his assignment</td><td></td><td></td></tr>
</table>

(Contd...)

Works efficiently	• Is he adaptable to unexpected changes		
Support level	• Does he understand team members' strengths and limitations in order to provide appropriate support		
Initiative	• Does he take initiative to plan and organize activities and tasks		
Collective ownership and problem-solving	• Whether he integrates information, expertise and skills from other team members to solve problems of simple to medium complexity		

Group Accountability Level

The Group Accountability Level worksheet enables to ascertain whether subgroups within teams work collectively and take up ownership collectively too. The various factors in the worksheet assess the level of positive interdependence in terms of roles, tasks, knowledge, support and feedback within teams. All of these factors finally map onto collaborative accountability.

Names of the Team Members: Roles and Responsibilities shared: Tasks/Subtasks: Overall level of collective ownership, responsibility, learning, reward sharing: Team manager's comments:			
Factors	Specific examples/ methods/ incidents	Facilitative team members	Specific pointers for team members with low to medium level of accountability
Explore and encourage the value of collective ownership			
Level of role interdependence co-shared			
Level of task interdependence co-shared			
Cooperative learning habits			
Degree of goal sharing			
Ways in which team members exhibit group accountability by integrating individual accountability with positive interdependence			
Acceptance level and reaction type to peer assessments			

5.4.3 *Advantages of Accountability*

A. Helps team members to earn the trust of co-workers.

B. Leads to more accuracy of work, vigilant problem-solving and effective decision-making.

C. As each person is entrusted with a fair level of accountability, he knows what it takes to discharge the responsibilities. Hence, there is greater appreciation for the contributions of others.

D. Leads to a sense of responsibility and collective ownership, which motivates team members to take up assignments even outside their assigned scope of duties. This leads to increased flexibility in task assignments.

E. Team members have a certain amount of control over each others' behavior; this control builds positive peer pressure, thereby cutting down the bureaucratic aspect of it. Each team member takes feedback in a positive sense because each member knows that he too has the right to give feedback. Accountability is not a one way lane; it has space both for receiving and giving feedback.

F. There is greater cooperation among workers. This advantage stems from the previous point.

5.5 Manage Results—'Bring About Super Success'

Team up to achieve results
So that everyone exults.

Is your team performing at its full potential? Rationalizing poor performance is the biggest hurdle in managing results. Managing results is as challenging as managing people who bring about those results. Do I hear "I agree" echoes skittering across in the background? Here's a checklist of the ways needed for managing results.

5.5.1 Team Development Plans—'Clear Definition'

There has to be a way in which individual team members forge a high performance team. This is exactly done by a team development plan. It creates an environment whereby everyone feels comfortable in communicating their success, sharing their concerns and throwing up their challenges. The quicker success is shared, the quicker it flows to others, thereby strengthening the bonds. The quicker challenges are aired, the quicker they are solved.

Apart from the regular issues of rewards, individual training needs and team training goals, the team development plan includes information on how to integrate best practices to build result-driven teams. The exact process of measuring results as against performance baselines is detailed out in the plan too.

5.5.2 Clear Context—'The Basics'

Clear context drives people towards focused performance. Answers to the questions given below, realize a clear context for functioning and achieving results:

Who we are -> Values

Where we are -> What is the current stage

Where we are heading to -> Vision and purpose

How we will get there - > Plans and strategies

Have we got there yet -> Evaluation, performance review

How we have performed and achieved the results -> Praise/Reprimand

Clear context creates a collective sense of belonging and connectedness.

5.5.3 Recognition—'Do it Well'

Recognition is the fuel needed to lubricate the wheels of an SDWT and to keep it in momentum. Two of the most effective ways of ensuring that teams never falter from the path of performance are:

1. Tie rewards and compensation to team performance.
2. Management provisions for teams to have their deserving share in the financial success of the organization.

If you want team members to behave in a certain way and they do perform as expected, they need to be recognized and rewarded. If team members give low performance or don't perform at all, then they need to be re-mentored. Regular sessions of celebrating milestones and accomplishments reinforce hard work put in by a team, time and again.

Along with celebrations, a team performance profile needs to be created for ongoing assessment and evaluation in regards to the results achieved. Typically, such a profile encompasses information derived from surveys, audits and progress reviews. They gather inputs based on several performance parameters—individual performance, team performance, and management support. Taking these inputs into consideration, a team is able to analyze its current performance, highlight key issues and modify the action plans accordingly.

5.5.4 Experimentation Pays—'Enable Adaptability'

A team and its team manager need to give up on the habit of clinging to unrealistic objectives. They need to learn to take up and commit to the appropriate objectives based on the situation they are facing.

One of the most important reasons for team failure is reluctance to sacrifice best-case scenarios in order to reach the final goal. Teams fail to understand that the best case scenarios may be the best bet only on paper. There can be more lucrative alternatives given the current set of constraints.

Experimentation along with a 360-degree view of the challenges is very important to ensure that advantageous alternatives are identified, studied, and feedback from all ends is received.

5.5.5 Effective Leadership Teams—'Leaders with a Team Player Attitude'

The top executives along with team managers must spend quality time with each team in working out improvement strategies, long-term goals, practical policies and strategic directions. This goes to reinforce the fact that teams and top management both are equally involved and interested in not just short-term immediate results, but are also oriented towards long-term growth. Thus, team members feel reassured that they are going to be needed even after the current project is completed, and in the process they become highly self-driven in order to meet the goals. Both the parties need to set new goals that are aligned with the team's purpose and the organizational mission so that they become a permanent continuous improvement team that is constantly adding value.

5.5.6 Proper Sequencing of Work—'Organized Work Improves Clarity Drastically'

Proper sequencing and structuring of work is of crucial importance for achieving the results. It is related to identification of tasks, interdependencies, and constraints in the form of time, scope and cost.

Team members need to be involved while defining the project scope and success criteria. Apart from this, their inputs are required while defining each of the phases, and its activities and tasks.

By involving team members in these critical stages of project development, ensures that they have professional obligation towards the completion of each of the phases and finally the end result (the project) as well.

5.5.7 Business Plans—'The Perfect Pitch'

The overall business strategy ascertains team goals and what steps have to be taken to achieve these goals. The plan also accounts for what each team member must do to implement this plan. Team members also require their own personal marketing plans. Each team member's plan sets out the details of the contribution that he needs to make to his team's overall success. Sharing these plans with the customers, reposes customer's confidence in the quality of output. These plans create a strategic link between teams and their customer, thereby creating opportunities for immediate customer feedback.

This kind of feedback loop resets goals in order to meet the revised customer expectations and strategies, thereby avoiding any deviation from the results baseline.

5.5.8 Supportive Leadership—'Proactive Management'

When it comes to people, the big difference is leadership, to be more precise 'effective managers'. When a self-directed team operates, it not only needs to be supported by management, but it also needs team managers who are willing to take on the necessary responsibility and be held accountable.

This means both the ends have to work in tandem to produce the desired results, only then shared leadership in the true sense will come to be.

SDWTs perform at the peak level, only when they have a *reasonable* degree of choice. Every team manager needs to be benevolent enough to respect and encourage his team's decisions. Initiative-driven work, free from unnecessary managerial intervention is the building block for excellent results.

5.5.9 Example—'The Star Scapegoat'

Problem Statement

At a coffee break session, two colleagues were discussing the monthly staff meeting. "Jen, what happened you look furious," asked a concerned Ryan. "I am totally taken aback; our team manager took away all the credit for my business proposal. He didn't even bother to appreciate me after the meeting" replied Jen, dismally. Jen continued to tell Ryan that she had gone to meet the team manager post meeting and how he scoffed her that she was always fishing for compliments which she did not deserve at all. "He said that it's my job to write business proposals and take all the blame if things go wrong. I have to play the star scapegoat as long as I make him look good at meetings and that's what I get paid for. I really don't feel motivated to work anymore and I feel hopeless within. Team work is all about supportive leadership, team development and recognition, but for our team manager we are nothing and he is everything", retorted Jen.

Problem Analysis

Jen's team manager is non-supportive and non-facilitative. He believes in the dictatorial style of leadership. His cold attitude is the main reason for the dissatisfaction and hopelessness experienced by his team.

Jen did approach her team manager to sort things out, but his non-cooperative attitude and false accusations put her off to such an extent that she does not feel like contributing any more. She has come to realize that her ideas and proposals are not going to be recognized.

Solution

As I have mentioned earlier that the onus of developing a healthy team climate and managing results lies on a team manager. Unless team managers express their supportive behavior through their actions and decisions, their team is definitely not going to exhibit the same kind of behavior.

Every team manager must express personal gratitude for outstanding performance rather than using derogatory remarks. By doing so, he makes himself accessible to discuss team development and enhancement plans. His encouraging testimonials give his team an impetus to put in more. It is vital for each manager to acknowledge and openly appreciate new ideas and proposals in the meeting. A team manager who steals limelight from deserving team members is a sure shot way of discouraging team members.

Each and every team manager needs to see beyond the monetary aspect of recognition, and develop appropriate recognition measures and business plans that keep his team motivated throughout.

5.5.10 Worksheet for Managing Results

Results Evaluation

The Results Evaluation worksheet provides an excellent quick reference of expected versus actual results, gap analysis, resolution tips and team members responsible for the same. This worksheet can be used to report progress for a particular reporting period.

RESULTS EVALUATION FOR THE PERIOD: For each item below, use the scale given below to rate it 1 = Below the mark, 2 = Needs further analysis, 3 = Results achieved almost always, 4 = As expected, 5 = Beyond expectations					
Module/Tasks	Sub Tasks	Team Members responsible	Expected (Date and % complete)	Actual (Date and % complete)	Gap Analysis and action tools

(Contd...)

Inputs from the team members:
Are the results evaluation tools fair, accurate and simple:
Is the results data collected and shared in a fair manner:
To be filled in by the team manager:
Results summary:
Lessons learned:
Comments and recommendations:
Overall rating:

5.5.11 Advantages of Managing Results

A. Team members are enthusiastic about their work and there is a common commitment towards the results. More time is spent on strategically beneficial issues rather than unnecessary firefighting.

B. Noteworthy improvements are contributed by team members as they enjoy the confidence and support of top management.

C. There is improved buy-in in all decisions and agreements, thereby minimizing the time and effort spent on sorting out frictions.

D. Ongoing assessment becomes second nature of a team.

E. There is a spirit of cooperation rather than confrontation.

5.6 Chapter Recap

1. Proper team management techniques support teams in co-creating and co-sharing corporate success.
2. A positive environment and robust support mechanisms is a must for generating and sharing positive team energy. Guide your employees in understanding their organization and their role in it, in a better way, so that they can feel more motivated in their work, and develop a positive attitude towards their work and their fellow team mates.
3. It's important to encourage entrepreneurial thinking as it raises the level of team ownership. As a result of which, team members care more about their team due

to the personal sense of belonging. It is human nature to care more about something that you are a owner of.

4. The only way to distinguish between what is unrealistic vision and what is attainable reality is by having a well laid down team results management process. Once team processes and breakdowns are managed in an orderly fashion, results automatically come about.

6

The Quartet Approach of Collaboration—'The Magic Quadrants'

Expanding Paradigms—It's all about people,
It's all about being zestful
And it's all about being equal.

Today, pulling together teams is more than just a process, but rather it is a way of life for businesses. Organizations are putting in their level best to discover and nurture passionate resources rather than just viewing them as 9-5 employees. The OAR phases are three main phases of team development, but for these phases to be successful, the quartet approach of collaboration is crucial.

Finding the right mix of resources is very much possible, but it requires organizations to be brave enough to change the way they think about their employees. This transition in thinking patterns is possible with the quartet of collaboration workflow, which involves four main aspects: Thinking outside the box management, human factors, quality and fine tuned processes.

SDWTs fail, when there is a failure to motivate and respect human factors. Continual management support along with proper processes can generate human energy of a high quality. Organizations seeking the collaborative spirit of teams, strive to create a transparent teaming environment. Joint team meetings take the spirit of collaboration to the next level. It is about including cross-departmental teams, this is useful especially when the work of external teams is either dependent on your team's work or affects your team functions. To ensure smooth functioning amongst all departments, the management may need to initiate something called as bridge teams, which act as intermediary channels of information sharing, problem-solving and reporting links amongst all functional groups.

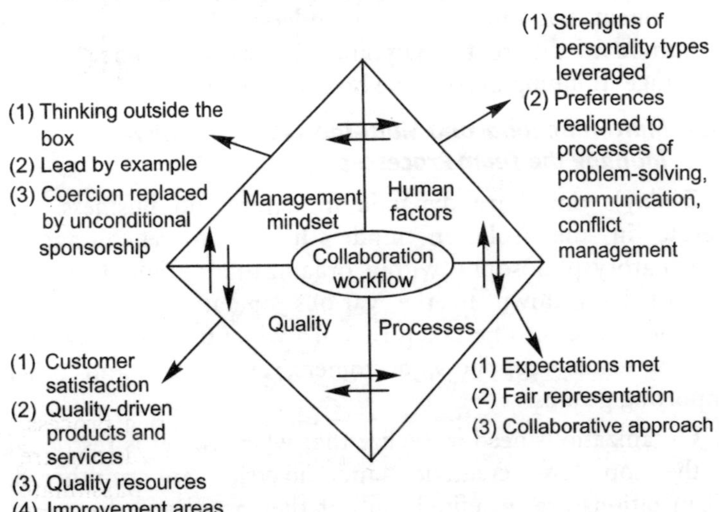

Fig. 6.1: The Collaboration Workflow

6.1 Top Management Mindset—'Create Global Managers'

Corporate performance
Is also dependent
On top management's performance.

The top rung executives are the ones who need to build dynamic strategies that in turn enable teams to contribute to continuous improvement and the ongoing success of organizations.

6.1.1 Thinking Outside the Box— 'Promote Fresh Perspectives'

Demonstrating teamwork at the topmost tier of an organization, promotes the culture of teams in terms of generation of creative ideas and multiple alternatives. It sets the pace for utilizing diverse experience to solve difficult problems, even in the offspring/satellite teams down the line.

No top executive can make the complex decisions that arise in today's competitive culture all by himself. These decisions require team synergy and the combined knowledge of many.

For tuning into the new trends of team building, the management not only needs to understand but also has to accommodate different viewpoints. It needs to practise and encourage 'thinking outside the box paradigm'.

6.1.2 *Multi-functional and Multi-faceted Philosophy—'Manage the Team Processes'*

Today's times are dynamic in nature; no business can operate in the isolation mode. It has to encourage a participatory philosophy within organizations, right from the topmost level down to the various operational tiers. The philosophy needs to be taken forward while forging links with external teams—suppliers, customers, end users, and other supporting groups.

Organizations need to realize that when power is restricted to the top few, creativity and diversity are smothered. Organizations are benefited, only if they are driven by teams and not by autocrat behavior.

Successful top level teams not only understand and appreciate the implications of their functions and duties, but also relate to the breadth of operations that occur in teams. Organizations have to ensure that team managers learn to wear many hats efficiently, knowing exactly when to don a particular hat and when to pull it off. The management needs to realize that team building is all about change management.

6.1.3 *Demonstrate Team Dynamics—'Focus on Decentralization'*

The top management needs to lead by example and practice, and not by force or rules. This encourages teams to replicate the behavior and values of the top management. They are inspired to contribute their committed efforts to the shared mission. A top management team which demonstrates desirable team dynamics and not power play leads to greater employee participation.

In order for the SDWTs to operate successfully, team managers need to act as a team resource rather than just as a facilitator or mediator. Working closely with a team, in a team and for a team, helps team managers to develop the attitude and skills needed to keep the momentum of a team going.

6.1.4 Example—'The Short-sighted Visionary'

Problem Statement

Martha, an excellent visionary who had contributed a lot to building a great image for her organization was somehow not a people's manager. To maintain her stronghold, she treated her employees as paid slaves. Her efforts for building great corporate level relationships are laudable, but as far as adapting to team dynamics was concerned, she had not spent much time in enhancing her skills.

For Martha, teamwork was nothing but mere slogging out without a break, and this had started showing detrimental impact on employees and their performance levels. They didn't feel motivated or committed at all, as their needs were not being taken care of.

Problem Analysis

It is a clear case of lack of executive support and the presence of an autocratic style of leadership. As time goes by, team members are bound to realize that they are mere workers, and are not going to receive any encouragement in terms of career growth and personal development. This realization is going to affect the team's motivation level, and eventually the team manager too.

By building a barrier of superior-subordinate relationships, Martha is definitely inviting trouble. She has not realized that all her proposals were translated into results by her team. It is because of their incessant efforts that she had earned the status of a visionary, but her one man army attitude is pulling the team in a different direction. By doing so, she has failed to gain the trust of her team.

Solution

It is the responsibility of the top management to staff their organization with team managers who appreciate and implement the processes and tools that are required to create a caring organization. Training sessions are an important factor, to inculcate in them a caring attitude. A team manager must develop personal bonds with each of his team members, of course within the professional confines, to understand and encourage team members' aspirations and improvements plans.

The management needs to realize that the only way to earn the trust of their teams is to recognize them as team players and not merely as 9-5 workers. Formal authority needs to be replaced with participative philosophy; only then team members view their team managers as problem-solvers and not as problem creators.

All team managers must remember that the end result is a product of team work and not that of a team manager's vision. A team manager's vision is just a starting point but it is his team that translates it into success. Team managers must convey their pride in their team members and their accomplishments, on a regular basis. To get out of the typical mode of managing teams, the mindset of both team managers and top executives needs to transmute into a dynamic, outside the box thinking style.

6.1.5 Worksheet for Top Management Mindset

Top Management Outlook

The Top Management Outlook worksheet assists each team manager and his team in pinpointing whether lack of top management direction is one of the potential causes of team failure. A team manager can distribute such worksheets to his team members for collating their responses to analyze the situation better. He too can fill up the worksheet. The same worksheet can be used to find out whether or not a team manager himself believes in the participatory philosophy of teams.

Team Member Name: Team Member's Comments: Team Manager's Key Notes: For each factor below, use the scale given as under to rate it 1 = Never, 2 = Rarely, 3 = Almost always, 4 = As expected, 5 = Beyond expectations			
Factors	Description	Response	Rating
Networking	• Does top management focus on only local networking or also supports both local/ global networking • Whether management provides scope for new, independent directions to the teams		
Balance of power	• Whether centralized and concentrated or decentralized • Is corporate energy directed and managed to achieve high team performance		
Accountability to employees	• Is there an increased level of accountability towards employees		
Code of ethics	• Whether the top management mindset exemplifies the ideal behavior of complying with code of ethics and standard operating procedures		
Role models	• Do the executives walk the talk		
Innovative reforms	• Are the reforms capable of ensuring long-term performance of the teams		
High-level decision-making	• Is decision-making readily delegated to team members		

(Contd...)

	• Are expert inputs taken from teams while designing the corporate agenda		
Opportunities	• Are teams given chances to acquire more skills and competencies • Are opportunities for upward mobility and global assignments given to teams		
Diversity affinity	• How much do the top managers value multicultural diverse teams		
Flexibility	• Does the organization give space for creativity and experimentation		

6.2 Processes—'Create a Dynamic Portfolio of Results'

Processes lead to increased efficiency
And effectiveness.
Right from the first meeting to the final game
They create a network of harmony, ceaseless.

With the changes in team management models, smoothening out the processes is also required to fuse well with these changes. The success of a team-based structure depends on the extent to which team processes meet team members' growth and satisfaction needs. Top management needs to make the right process choices to bring about harmony in the collaboration workflow, right from the first meeting to the final game. The leadership process affects the values, beliefs, and behaviors of team members, which goes to show that leadership processes and team processes are closely linked.

Expectations of the various stakeholders involved in the project—top management, business owners, customers, team managers and team members decide upon the processes. The main factors required for defining the processes:

A. Processes related to values and behaviors of team stakeholders.

B. Expectations of each team member from the other, expectations of a team manager and expectations of top management.

C. The various tools and techniques for building teams.

To make any process a success, the SDWT needs to take into account the worst case scenario too. This acts as a hedge against the future, by identifying and clarifying the worst possible outcome, if anything were to go wrong. It helps a team to prepare itself to face the negative outcome with equal confidence, just as it would face the best case scenario. Another advantage of spotting worst case scenarios is that it allows a team to thoroughly analyze the underlying assumptions and come up with more accurate data to minimize risks.

The three main processes are: Problem-solving, Conflict Management and Decision-making

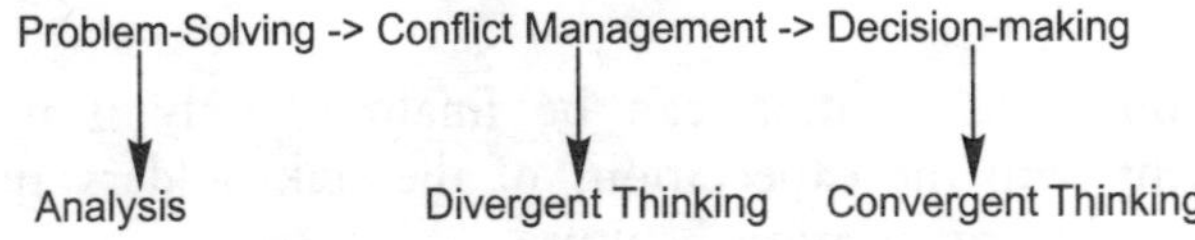

6.2.1 *Problem-solving—'No More Thinking Traps'*

Problem-solving is the most important process as it provides direction for taking crucial decisions.

The most important aspect of problem-solving is a common definition of the problem statement. Innovation is another important subpart of problem-solving, as turning any undesirable condition to a desirable condition requires a creative approach. Each organization needs to provide access to books, electronic media, discussion forums, field trips and training to stimulate new perspectives.

The gravity of the problem has a major influence on the way of solving it. At times, the problem is a small hitch in the day-to-day activity of a team. Here 2-3 team members or even a single team member can work out the solution. All that needs to be taken care of is that the other aspects of a team should not be impacted, in short, there must not be any cascade effect on a team and its functional areas.

For complex problems involving technical, management, or social issues, there needs to be a team meeting where people discuss the problem, implement critical thinking, and expert opinion is also solicited. There is a thorough analysis process before selecting and implementing the best alternative, in line with a team's guiding principles, values and stakeholders' expectations. The problem is solved based on a team's collective judgment and functional expertise.

A problem is approached by breaking it into manageable sub-units. Decomposition facilitates the process of analyzing the cause and effect. After this analysis is complete, team members are able to single out the gaps in a much better way. Team members come up with several alternatives based on the chunks, and try to modify them to get rid of the negative causes and effects. This process is cyclic in nature and they have to loop through it several times before arriving at the solution.

A proposed solution can be finalized, only if it is in alignment with the expectations of the stakeholders and fits well with the organizational culture.

6.2.2 Conflict Management—'Encourage Each Other'

There is one important step between the problem-solving and decision-making processes—Conflict management. Once the problem is analyzed and all the underlying assumptions are discussed, a team needs to come up with alternatives. Alternatives are nothing but products of different thinking styles within a team, and they are a vital component for enhancing the culture of constructive conflict.

Analysis of alternatives which are produced by divergent thinking leads to conflict. A proper guideline in place for solving conflicts in a healthy way, aids a team in arriving at a lucrative consensus. A team manager must encourage everyone to air their views and opinions. This form of divergent analysis lets team members categorize and discuss issues from various angles. This ensures that people learn to recognize and benefit from their differences.

Various views and suggestions also help to arrive at an alternative which aligns with organizational goals and ensures that no core processes are affected negatively.

6.2.3 Decision-making—'Generate Quality Decisions'

A decision is nothing but the selection of one alternative from a number of options. This is where convergent thinking comes into play. Convergent thinking is applied to each of the alternatives to pinpoint their strengths, weaknesses, opportunities and threats, and then a rational choice is arrived at. As the collective role of a team was encouraged in the earlier two processes, by the time a team reaches this process, it automatically plays it.

Decision-making refers to the selection of one or more value-driven alternatives produced during the conflict management process. Decision-making is a process which helps team members to hone their judgment skills and learn from each other. Collective judgment plays a key role in determining the aftermath of a decision. The higher the positive rating, the more likely the decision is both agreed upon and implemented. Decisions are needed to strike a balance between the short-term and long-term effects faced by an organization, and also ensure that all stakeholders have fair representation in the decision. Any decision taken finally translates into value addition. The more value it is going to add to the product/service, the more likely it is going to be implemented. Just as in the case of problem-solving, a team needs to ensure that there is no negative effect on other areas and processes, similarly in case of decisions too, a team has to ensure that the decision affects only those areas that fall in its scope.

There are several factors that contribute to the process of arriving at a quality decision. The most important factor is the mission statement; remember I had mentioned earlier that the mission is the main bonding factor for any team. This mission ensures that there are no unnecessary conflicts. Mission statement coupled with leadership efficiency of steering the decision-making process in the right direction makes a big difference. The second most important factor that needs to be analyzed for its aftermath is the risks involved in the decision. They need to be studied and planned for. Apart from this, other elements like team member expertise and accuracy of information also matter. Timing of the decision also affects the implementation strategy. There is no point in implementing a high quality decision, if its effectiveness is going to be lost due to delays or imperfect conditions in an organization. At times, team members disagree on certain aspects of the decision; it is here that brainstorming comes into picture. Brainstorming over disagreements is vital for bringing out all of the information.

A decision is likely to be taken by a team member on his own, if it is related to a day-to-day activity, and then he communicates it to his team members and shares the reason behind the decision. In case of complex high risk decisions, team members indulge in convergent thinking. A formal meeting is held for arriving at the decisions based on various inputs from other technical experts, stakeholders, team manager. When organizational policies or operating procedures are concerned, the decisions are taken by the management, and the concerned team is kept well informed and rationale for management's final decision is also shared with team members. Keeping a team well informed is a must for both building and sustaining the 'self-directed' setting.

The main aim of having precisely characterized processes in a team are objectivity, meeting of expectations and equal participation by all team members.

6.2.4 Example—'Mission Decision'

Problem Statement

Tim, a team manager in a software team conducted an anonymous feedback for acquiring information on the decision-making process of the team. After analyzing the survey results, he was shocked to read many negative comments, for example, "The term decision is something I really can't relate to", "Decision making is not in my dictionary", "Our inputs are not solicited and we hardly trust the management and its prudence." Tim knew exactly where the problem lies and that some concrete measures would be needed to remodel this negative attitude of the employees.

Problem Analysis

The team manager realizes that by not considering valuable inputs of his team members, the concerned organization is losing out on dynamic intelligent energy. As the organization is not paying heed to the collective wisdom, the employees do not feel trusted. They feel that the organization is only interested in financial figures and not in the employee growth factor. They feel left out from the decision-making process, and hence do not feel like contributing.

Solution

The most important factor for earning the trust of team members is to trust them and their inputs. Executives and team managers need to acknowledge and appreciate new suggestions, models and proposals from team members. Soliciting team inputs while arriving at decisions is crucial, at least in the case of decisions that pertain to team members directly. Controlling each and every decision of a team is detrimental to any organization. Each team must be given every opportunity to self-direct their work, as long as they perform in accordance to the mission.

Management must realize that complex decisions have a large risk associated with them. They need to accept the reality of limited options, but at the same time appreciate that team inputs also make the process of decision-making less painful and minimize risks. This attitude is essential as management is not an expert in all fields. On several occasions, team managers have to make a decision outside their knowledge zone, and the best way to arrive at a feasible decision is by considering expert opinions from team members.

Explicit and measurable ground rules governing the decision-making process need to be prescribed to and monitored by a team manager, in conjunction with team inputs. Buy-in from all the stakeholders is extremely important to bring about participative decision-making.

6.2.5 Worksheets for Processes

Problem-solving

The Problem-solving worksheet fosters a team collaboration attitude towards addressing the problems that a team faces. The worksheet can be used to capture all aspects related to the problem, right from problem attributes to action plans and monitoring details.

Problem statement:

Definition:

Goal of the problem-solving exercise:

Desired outcomes and baseline measures:

Details:

(A) What are the symptoms:

(B) When was the problem first noticed:

(C) Who are the stakeholders and how are they affected:

(D) What are the root causes:

(E) What are the most damaging aspects:

(F) What is the trend of occurrence—random, continuous, cyclical:

(G) What are the organizational barriers:

(H) What corrective measures can be taken to minimize the risk element:

(I) List the data and documents that may assist you to define the problem more exactly:

(J) Preventing recurrence action tools:

(K) How much will problem correction cost in terms of people, money and time:

Problem description is either included as a flow diagram or a cause and effect diagram:

(Contd...)

Possible Solutions:

Option 1: <Description>

Positive Outcomes:

Negative Outcomes:

Option 2: <Description>

Positive Outcomes:

Negative Outcomes:

Action Plan Details:

What are the most difficult, complex aspects of the plan:

Will any technical, human-related issues hamper the plan:

Sub-plan details	Responsibility	Completion Planned Actual	Status

Action Plan Tracking:

Team members responsible	What plans have been implemented	Results (whether satisfactory or not)	Completion status	Likely date of completion

Monitoring Details:

What will be monitored/measured:

How will it be monitored/measured:

When and how often it will be monitored/measured:

Findings of previous follow-up:

Conflict Management Action Plan

The Conflict Management Action Plan worksheet not only identifies the common causes of conflict, but also ensures that each team member gets equal opportunity to share his views and responses, which can turn out to be valuable inputs for eliminating conflicts.

Reporting Team Member Name:

Conflict Description:

Involved Team Members:

(Contd...)

Likely causes and symptoms:

"Hot button" issues:

Team members involved	Differences in interests/ points of view	Possible areas where there could be the most and least level of agreement	Ready to negotiate/ discuss	Likely reactions and responses

Do you think the assumptions of reasons for the conflict are real or perceived:

What is your exact attitude towards team members involved in this conflict:

What worries you most about this conflict:

Are there any objective criteria that can be used to find common ground, if yes describe them:

What are the common needs:

Which needs are in conflict:

Do you see this conflict as an opportunity:

Possible workaround and what will be your inputs to it:

What steps can you take if other team members refuse to negotiate:

What criteria do you think can be used to evaluate the fairness of the workaround:

Anticipated results:

Decision-making

The Decision-making worksheet lets the SDWT to study factors that help team members to choose the best possible alternative to arrive at the final decision.

Decision details and objectives:

Key stakeholders:

Time table that will be used to collect input and share the findings:

In the "Importance" column, rate how important the factor is for the decision on a scale of 1-5.

(Contd...)

1 = not very important

5 = highly important

In the "Probability" column, rate the likelihood that the factor will be fulfilled if a particular option is chosen:

1 = least probable

5 = highly probable

Note*: Multiply the Importance by the Probability and record that into the Sub-total column for each alternative. Add the subtotals for each column and enter the total at the bottom underneath each alternative. Compare the totals of each alternative and the one which has the highest value could be your best bet.

Alternative 1: <description>

Pros (short-term and long-term):

Cons (short-term and long-term):

Factors	Importance	Probability	Sub-total	Additional Notes—known issues, risks, legal restrictions, etc.
Resources needed:				
Amount of funding				
Organizational backing				
Skills and expertise on the team				
Technology and training needs				
Outside consultants				
Comfort level of the team				
Level of administrative support				
Returns:				
Value addition				
Cost saving				
Time saving				

(Contd...)

Controlled risk				
Effectiveness				
Learn something new along the way				
Build a sense of community				
Work Values:				
Develop expertise				
Career development				
Innovativeness/ Creativity				
Mental challenges				
Stakeholder expectations:				
Buy-in from key stakeholders				
Level of involvement				
Satisfying stakeholder interests				
Total:				
Rationale: Reasons for: Reasons against: Possible consequences: Primary concerns: Role of timing factor: Best Case Scenario: Worst Case Scenario:				

6.3 Quality—'Succeed Through Enriched Resources'

Quality human energy is the driving force
Behind the success of organizations,
Which in turn creates
Happy customers in the count of millions.

The key to ensuring quality of an SDWT involves monitoring, measuring and modifying the behaviors of individual team members. Team managers have to constantly keep a check on team members and their adherence levels to the established quality standards. Quality standards are various performance indicators that need to be followed in order to produce quality output. Team members can also self-audit and correct their discrepant actions along with their team manager's review inputs. Quality must become a habit and to sustain it, time and training are required.

There are three steps in analyzing the quality level of a team:

A. **Identification**—Collect and measure the metrics related to work.

B. **Analysis**—Study the metrics collected to list out the issues.

C. **Action**—Design action plans to correct behavior and to preserve the standards.

The top management has to play a perfect role model for creating a great quality-driven team. The top management has to display three main characteristics in order for a team to follow in their footsteps: Credit sharing, honesty and positive attitude.

6.3.1 Quality Areas—'Reliable Resources, Reliable Results'

The quality aspect of a team encompasses the areas given as follows:

The End Product/Service Offered

The value of the end products/services is derived based on their quality factor—Reliability. Reliability represents the quality of the products/services in terms of how well it works. Reliability has to be built into the products/services right from day one and checked for consistency throughout the development. Organizations cannot afford to have reliability as an after the fact process as this would cost them heavily due to the rework involved, and this in turn could lead to loss of goodwill and customer trust. Team members have to be coached to satisfy quality procedures, customer specifications, and standards founded for the various development stages of products/services.

Team Members

Quality is not limited to the end product and its features, or merely customer satisfaction. Over the years, organizations have realized the importance of enhancing the quality of the people in a team. They are no more looked at as mere workforce who do what they are told to do. Rather now, organizations ensure that proper provisions are made for improving the quality level for all activities that the workforce takes up, right from conducting meetings to designing solutions.

Customer Expectations

Team members need to perform in such a way that the expectations of the customer are met. Every action of each team member has to maintain focus on fulfilling customer needs.

Customers come back to an organization for more products/services, only when they are given a quality-driven product/service. Quality is an important differentiator, when it comes to selecting the right vendor/supplier/manufacturer. If the quality is remarkably high, then the customer does not mind paying a high cost for the same. Another aspect that retains customers is the level of quality in the communication that occurs between team members and customers. Timely, accurate and definitive responses to customer queries and suggestions, strengthen the ties between both the parties.

6.3.2 Quality Circles and Statistical Quality Control—'A Wide Spectrum of Advantages'

There can be no overnight success where quality is concerned. Regular weekly meetings provide a forum to discuss, improvise, and document quality and quality monitoring checkpoints. The findings can be used for future use. This is where quality circles come into play. A quality circle is a team in itself, which is empowered to promote and bring the quality improvements through to fruition.

Quality circles when given the right top management commitment, they can bring about continuous quality improvement. Every team is able to diagnose issues and find a solution to any issue that hampers the quality; the issue could be related to work allocation or even day-to-day communication, or anything else that is related to a team.

There are various techniques that can be used for correcting deviances—process flow charts, pareto analysis, brainstorming and a whole lot of others. More than the technique, what is important, is that team members need to be trained to implement these techniques depending on the issue that they are handling. They should be capable of choosing the right method for the given context.

Statistical quality control refers to gathering statistics about a particular problem, and how it is being addressed and corrected to meet the desired quality level. This problem could be a technical one or could occur at individual or team level. The statistics have to be collected in an empirical manner so as to eliminate human biases. These statistics, if shared and discussed, help a team to develop strategies in accordance with the gravity of the quality issue. These statistics also allow team members to pinpoint quality improvement areas.

Any process which is governed by team behavior and values has certainly an output to it. The quality of this output is based on certain attributes and an acceptable range of deviation. Any variance between the actual and expected that falls beyond the set range calls for immediate correction. Statistical quality control enables a team to focus on baselines and quality enhancement capabilities.

Training and vigilant mentoring is the key to successful implementation of quality circles and process control methods.

6.3.3 Worksheet for Quality Process

Quality Review

The Quality Review worksheet gives a snapshot of what has been done, what is in progress and what needs to be done, in order to successfully implement all the quality-related criteria and processes in an SDWT.

Process/Criteria	In place	Needs fine tuning	Yet to implement	Facts and figures	Level of priority
Quality control processes both developed and documented					
Quality aspects related to team members, customer expectations and product specifications are in place and updated as per change in requirements					
Procedures for self-evaluation and team manager's evaluation of team quality are well defined and strictly adhered to					
Responsibility for quality processes is properly assigned					
Results of quality control are well documented					
Inputs from all the concerned stakeholders are solicited while developing quality-related processes, standards and criteria					
Implementation of new standards is monitored					

(Contd...)

regularly and the status of the same is shared with the concerned stakeholders					
Quality standards and processes reflect the team culture and organizational ethos					

6.4 Human Factors—'The Crux of Team Spirit'

Human Factors Make or Break an SDWT

Over the years, the study of human factors has extended beyond ergonomics, and entered into the realm of team behaviors as it relates to organizational growth.

Human factors are all about having an integrated system to develop the individual team members and the SDWT on the whole. The thinking outside the box concept must flow towards processes applied to human factors as well. Careful thought for human factors is necessary, as they aim at having a steady focus on the positive value of diversity. Trust and positive perspective provides a common platform, which speeds up concern-solving and facilitates detailed feedback for individual career and team development. The three main human factors that need to be taken into consideration are: **Team member types,** SWOT and **behavioral management.** These aspects are related to the soft side of business.

A shift in values, rise in awareness and a transformation in the way teams work leads to high-performance, spirited teams.

6.4.1 Team Member Types–'Unity Lies in Diversity'

Efficient SDWTs need to have a neat balance of team member types. Knowing the various team member types, enables to understand what makes them tick. When there is a good balance of these types, a team can exercise a balance in its operations, and that greatly improves the performance. Optimum success requires all of the team member types, with each being used in turn. When teams work together efficiently, it means team members have been able to recognize and use valuable individual differences to their advantage.

Remember the team formation phases—the sub-phase 3 of growth through acceptance is important as far as identifying team member types is concerned. It is here that the behavioral expectations and ground rules are identified. It is during this sub-phase that the strengths, weaknesses, opportunities and threats are established so as to avoid personality clashes.

Determining these types lets you discover the differences, which in turn aids teams to incorporate the uniqueness of each team member. This uniqueness contributes to group performance, *phenomenally*.

Do you recall the five team member types…let me give you a hint…elements of Nature…'Perfect Configuration'…Bingo you are a bright spark. Allow me to recap the five types for you:

A. Down to Earth Members

B. Clear Water Members

C. Sure Fire Members

D. Fair Air Members

E. Sky High Members

Based on the above team member types, team managers need to list out team players, their dominant styles and preferences. Then they need to mentally rehearse how they are going to confront each type. Here, team managers need to handle not only personality preferences but also interpersonal differences, which I have discussed in the previous chapter.

Dealing with various team members types in an effective way assists:

A. Teams to deal with differences.

B. Team members to be able to look at themselves in relationship to others, their work and their environment, objectively.

C. Team members to improve the coping skills, thereby producing more win-win scenarios.

D. Team members to be able to find the answers to two most important questions:
   1. Does the team have the best personalities for executing the tasks?
   2. Are the differences adding any value to the overall contribution of the team?

There are four negative types of personalities that need to be dealt with vigilantly in order to maintain the eco-balance of an SDWT, they are as follows:

A. **Complainers**—these personalities complain just about anything, right from the meeting room ergonomics to team manager's speaking style. They need to be dealt with empathy. They need to be shown the positive aspects by making them feel valued. There is no point in arguing, what is required is convincing.

B. **Non-players**—are mostly the ones who either don't perform at all or have joined a team with a cross-purpose. Open and constant communication with them is needed. It is difficult to find their true motives, but a team manager has to have patience to work out alternatives.

C. **Manipulators**—personalities who use manipulative ways of disrupting the performance and thwart team manager's efforts to bring a team together. A team and its team manager must make it clear that they will not tolerate such manipulation.

D. **Pleasers**—they are the ones who over commit and show unrequited enthusiasm towards all tasks. The only way to deal with these people is to affirm their commitment in a formal manner, which in a way, lets them realize that over commitment is hampering not only their performance but also their team's performance.

6.4.2 Examples of Personality Preferences

Once team members understand the basic personality preferences under which people operate, they along with managerial inputs can begin to find ways to effectively work with opposite types.

For example, there could be a certain person in a team who possesses very good soft skills, but when it comes to communication, he likes dominating the airtime. He is of the opinion that he can talk and talk and others do not mind it, since he feels his talking is crucial. The concerned team manager needs to reset the ground rules of communication and make him understand that listening is of equal importance. Communication is a two-way process. His team mates need to make him understand that by communicating both ways, both he and his team mates will benefit.

Another example of conflict is a person who judges every little aspect of others. He needs to be mentored so that he learns to be open to others and their viewpoints as well.

6.4.3 SWOT: Strengths, Weaknesses, Opportunities and Threats—'The Right Things to Do'

Before setting a new vision or direction, it's always beneficial to begin by analyzing where you are right now. This new vision could be a new product or a new team process. SWOT analysis must always be used as a guide and not as a prescription. In SWOT, strengths and weaknesses are internal factors, whereas opportunities and threats are external factors.

Simple rules that a team has to follow whether they are doing a SWOT for team members or for a particular situation that a team is facing are:

A. Be realistic about all the four aspects. Do not overestimate or underestimate them.

B. Keep it simple by avoiding unnecessary details.

C. Exhaust viewpoints and ideas for each aspect before moving to the next level.

D. Always conduct SWOT keeping in mind the current and past performance of a team.

SWOT goes hand in hand with brainstorming. The main purpose is to generate a huge list of ideas and opinions for each of the quadrant of the SWOT Matrix. It addresses two main questions, keeping in mind the expectations and goals of team members and their relation to the organizational growth:

A. What are the threats and opportunities present in the external marketplace that have an impact on the human factors—for example, new competition?

B. What are the strengths and weaknesses of the human factors translated in terms of several other factors like quality of work, skills, lack of skills, personality clashes?

Table 6.1: Example of SWOT Analysis

Strengths—What's working well (Internal) Quality team processes for decision-making	Weaknesses—What are the loopholes (Internal) Not a very robust conflict resolution strategy
Opportunities—What areas can we tap into (External) New niche areas that team members can tap into and add to their expertise	Threats—What are the obstacles (External) New competition threatens the existence of the team

SWOT analysis prioritizes key items, which in turn leads to better solutions and strategies.

6.4.4 Behavioral Management—'Inventive Collaboration is the Key'

Behavioral management is all about setting norms and institutionalizing values that need to be lived by. The management needs to set team standards not only for performance, communication and conflicts, but also for behavior. Team behavior has to be one of the parameters for measuring the success index of the SDWTs. Behavioral management is not about evaluating one another merely on the basis of work. It goes beyond the physical dimensions of work.

Processes and benchmarks have to be put in place in order to reinforce the acceptable form of behaviors, and this in turn is dependent on the previous two factors (team member types and SWOT). Organizational success continues to depend on how people work and interact with each other.

Only when organizations reward and appreciate the right behavior, their teams perform well. Forcing people to fit a particular structure without any incentive usually backfires. Standardization is acceptable, only as long as it respects the individuality of each team member. These standardized operating procedures can become successful best practices, only when the human element is taken into consideration.

Behavioral management focuses not just on the job needs, but also caters to the emotional goals of the employees. It is of prime importance that organizations make adequate provisions for taking care of employees' expectations. Just as employees align themselves with organizational goals, similarly the top management needs to align itself to the employee aspirations.

6.4.5 Example—'Clash of the Titans'

Problem Statement

This is the third time in the past one week, Larry, a software developer, had not checked-in his work in the source code repository. Ben, another developer, whose module was linked to Larry's latest version had been affected adversely and he was lagging behind by three days. Ben had reported this hitch to his team manager, but his team manager did not pay heed to his concerns, as Larry and the team manager were college mates. The subsequent modules had also got affected and the cascade effect seemed to have no end in sight as Larry was not at all cooperating. Ben tried talking to Larry about this concern, but Larry's cold attitude and dominating style seemed to be getting the team nowhere. Moreover, Larry was taking everyone for granted as he was a close friend of the team manager.

Problem Analysis

From the above problem statement, we can clearly see a personality clash (for all the wrong reasons) resulting in negative conflicts. The concerned team manager is not managing his resources well, and moreover, he is absolutely unfair in his attitude by adopting favoritism. By showing favoritism, he is polluting the team culture. He also does not realize the importance of planning, monitoring the resources and their work for qualitative correctness.

Another repercussion of the team manager not reorienting Larry's behavior is that Larry has begun to consider himself as the pseudo boss of the team. The excessive accommodation shown by the team manager towards Larry, makes him develop a non-player attitude and gives him the confidence to ignore the team. Due to this attitude, he treats Ben's request as trivial, and is not bothered about what the entire team is going through.

Solution

A truly bias-free workplace demands that everyone, regardless of the background, be given the recognition and respect they deserve. In case of such a conflict, what is imperative for a team manager is concord and conciliation. A good amount of self-introspection prevents a team manager from falling into prejudice traps and makes him realize the value of solidarity.

Striking a balance between all the personalities on a team is the most basic demand of SDWTs. It is the responsibility of team managers not only to reinforce team behavioral patterns, but also to encourage others to correct faulty behaviors related to teamwork processes.

First, the team manager needs to call in Larry for a serious, non-friendly discussion and work out a plan for correction. Secondly, he needs to give him a period of one week for reorienting his personality with the team. After a weeklong observation, he needs to call in Ben for his feedback and based on Ben's inputs, he will need to decide the further course of action.

6.4.6 Worksheets for Human Factors

Team Dynamics

The Team Dynamics worksheet shows how a particular team member reacts, behaves and controls team dynamics. It singles out any management issues that need to be addressed.

The worksheet lets team members review their relationships and what is their compatibility level with each other.

Team Scenario 1: Description of behavior dynamics, personality preferences and clashes Reporting Team Member: Team Manager's Key observations: Team Members involved: Name 1, Name 2………..	
To be filled in by the reporting team member. (Rating: 1=Agree fully, 2=Agree slightly, 3=Neither Agree nor Disagree, 4=Disagree slightly, 5=Disagree strongly) 1. Team members give each other feedback 2. Decisions are fair 3. Conflicts are more constructive 4. Problems are shared openly 5. Information is shared in a timely manner 6. There are no violent outbursts 7. You are well informed of the aspects that directly affect your work 8. Team members speak and respond in the team language—'WE' 9. Team members set aside their needs for the betterment of the team 10. Team members' strengths compensate for your weaknesses To be filled in by the team manager in consultation with the team member:	
Analysis Item	**Description**
The problem and its source	
Which of the characteristics/ processes/values is the team compromising	
What could the team manager do to get the team back on track	
Which of the characteristics of healthy interdependence is the team not exhibiting	
What training, executive sponsorship, orientation tools are needed for getting team members on track	

Potential Team Members

The right mix of people on an SDWT is important. Answers to the questions in the Potential Team Members worksheet gauge the potential of each candidate in terms of skills, attitude, personality type, preferences.

Team Member Name: Job Title: Role: Overall Rating: Achievements: Predominant Personality Type: Team Manager's notes:	
Criteria	Description
Educational background, skill set, domain knowledge, attitudes	
Professional experience and professional certifications	
Management skills—time, decisions	
Motivation level	
Special training	

Team Member Personality Profile
Please put a check mark against the appropriate factor The team member: 1. Acts in a timely manner 2. Communicates in an articulate manner 3. Has long-term vision 4. Is both creative and practical 5. Is able to prioritize effectively 6. Is open to change 7. Is well organized and performs in a well coordinated manner 8. Offers support to others 9. Respects and appreciates the team's opinions. Can see how things look from others' points of view 10. Is able to strike balance between short and long-term needs 11. Gives all aspects the right level of consideration before taking action 12. Is trustworthy and looked up to as a role model

(Contd...)

Action Item	Team Manager Recommendations
Team member's skills, style and preferences	
Problem areas and their Behavioral analysis	
Development Plans	
Review and Support methods	
List at least three strengths and special abilities	
Positive and negative work habits	

6.5 Chapter Recap

1. Reshaping the employee mindset can only occur when the top management mindset is reshaped. It is essential for the top management to strongly believe that by synergizing collective thinking power, creativity and knowledge of every one in an organization, leads to superior and sustainable results.
2. Only when top management facilitates smooth process transitions, they are able to develop 'Champions of Change' at the team level.
3. Quality standards are various performance indicators that need to be followed in order to re-orient faulty team dynamics so that quality output is produced.
4. Human factors and their cohesion are the most critical factors in team effectiveness. A cohesive team demonstrates a spirit of togetherness and support for one another, which in turn motivates team members to address problems, make decisions and resolve conflicts.

7

Building a High Performing Team—'The Key to Continuous Growth'

Performance is about managing work,
Optimizing outcomes
And producing team players—the biggest perk
Of self-directed work teams.

7.1 The Performance Maturity Loop—'Extraordinary Breakthroughs'

Team performance is dependent on team discipline. The performance maturity loop is the key to team discipline.

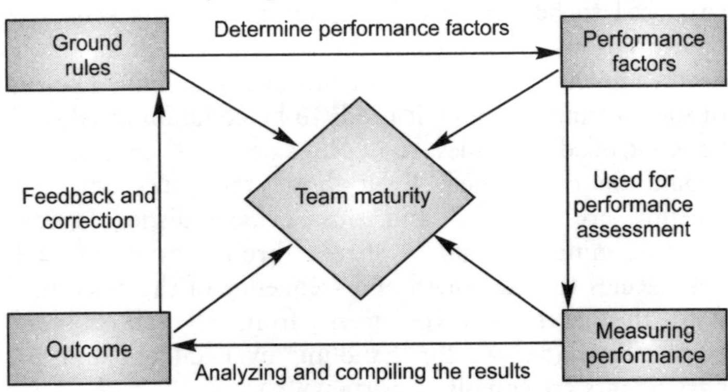

Fig. 7.1: The Performance Maturity Loop

After examining the SDWT's performance based on the performance factors, a team manager along with team inputs needs to understand where the focus for team improvement needs to be. This loop is not only about improving team performance, but also about individual enhancement and process optimization. It aims at integrating team and individual measurement so that they support each other.

7.2 Ground Rules—'Encourage Model Behavior'

Team members have got to play by the rules,
Which keeps them away from whirlpools.

Ground rules are ways of ensuring smooth workflow in SDWTs. They are a set of norms to guide teammates of "how to work together" in a team.

Ground rules must be detailed out at the very start, preferably at the kickoff meeting itself, in crystal clear terms. They have to clearly state what is expected from team members in order to avoid individual (mis)interpretations. The main areas which ground rules cover are:

A. Meetings

Rules for meetings include setting agenda, attendance criteria, timing, frequency and punctuality requirements. One example may be that the weekly status report meeting will be held on every Friday morning from 9 to 10 a.m. Apart from this, the conduct of teammates during the meeting, is also supposed to be governed by norms that clearly state that no one discusses issues outside the set criteria. All agenda items need to be discussed within the meeting time limit. The content of the meeting and how it needs to be communicated ought to be controlled by rules too. No side talks or interruptions should be entertained. Even 'how' the proceedings of the meeting are recorded and shared have distinct guidelines. Meeting minutes could be shared through printouts or by e-mail. Rules for the length and frequency of the meeting along with the level of involvement from all stakeholders are essential. Guidelines for handling over talkers and passive participants are equally important.

B. Team Member Relationships

Relationships are about co-sharing the same space in harmony. Clear rules have to be stated when it comes to team relationships:

1. Being open and honest
2. Sharing of ideas
3. Supporting each other
4. Encouraging breakthrough thinking
5. Empathy
6. Collaborative problem handling

C. Feedback

Procedures need to be devised such that a team member's feedback carries as much weight as a team manager's feedback. This can be done by instituting a team review process or making provisions in the performance appraisal system to include input from customers and team members as well. Even while making ground rules, the involvement needs to come from all parties; it is not merely a team manager activity.

D. Conflict Management

The key to having conflict resolution ground rules is to ensure that there is equal involvement from all stakeholders. Clear norms ensure that a team focuses on the issue and not on any particular team member.

When two or more team members consider themselves fit for the same role, this leads to overlapping roles and eventually to major conflicts. A team manager needs to clarify each team member's functional role, its boundary and extent of ownership in order to eliminate role conflict.

E. Effective Leadership

Team manager has to play an active role in building up a high performance team. In fact, he is the key person in setting up the appropriate climate for team members. The level of his involvement, right from the kickoff meeting through the formation stages of a team to other serious areas like conflict management, decision-making, plays a substantial role in determining team success. He needs to be open to receiving feedback on his leadership style. Every team manager must lead by example, and give feedback when the rules are adhered to and when they are ignored as well.

Team managers must have the tact to invoke the power of group mentality and leverage it for all team-related processes; this lets a team to perform as a self-directed autonomous unit. They feel ensured that they are not being sidelined and are endowed with a sense of ownership. Constancy of purpose has to be the forte of team managers. Team managers ought to commit themselves to the performance of their team, and not give up when the going gets rough.

F. Performance Measurement

An effective performance measurement system includes reviewing organizational processes, defining team measurement checkpoints, team reward standards, measuring and analyzing team success, and finding gaps using performance tracking. Precise rules have to be formulated for the above points. Team members also need to be briefed regarding the rules that need to be conformed to while conducting peer reviews.

Rating individual performance undermines collaboration; hence performance of a team must be given utmost importance.

G. Communication

Communication is about sharing of views and ideas on any topic pertaining to team dynamics, right from meeting place selection to performance assessment. Rules regarding the following mentioned aspects, facilitate a non-disruptive communication flow:

1. Equal participation.
2. Objective discussion. There is no room for criticism.
3. A favorable atmosphere.
4. Developing proper communication tools.
5. Have transparency and due respect for each team member.
6. Teammates encourage each other's creativity.

7. Manage misunderstandings, and be clear on ensuring agreement and clarity.

For any group to effectively work and perform as an SDWT, they need an understanding of what is expected of them, how decisions are to be made and how problems are to be resolved. At the same time, a team is required to document what will be the consequence for a team member who violates any of the above mentioned norms. As a team takes part in developing the ground rules related to all these aspects, this makes the rules more easily enforceable.

7.2.1 Example—'The Cascade Effect'

Problem Statement

Shaun, a dynamic module lead respected and liked by his team, is a star performer and a prospective project lead. He was having a conversation about his promotion with his colleague who was a senior business analyst. "Shaun, I heard that Rick your current project lead is quitting and you will be taking his place," asked Shaun's colleague. "Yea...After five years of loyal service, finally, I am getting what I deserve," said Shaun in an excited tone. "Are you sure of all this Shaun?," asked his colleague hesitatingly. This question did ring an alarm in Shaun's ears. "Yes...but why do you ask such a question?" His colleague goes on to tell him that he heard Shaun's manager speaking to his manager about appointing the newcomer in Shaun's team as the new project lead, "I thought you knew about these developments." "Hold on! You are telling me that the newcomer will be given consideration over me. My team manager never ever mentioned anything about this to me; rather he always gave me subtle cues about my promotion. If all this is true, then this time I am going to call it quits and that too for good."

Problem Analysis

Shaun's team manager has not being open and honest with Shaun. At the same time, Shaun has also committed the mistake of taking indirect cues as a promise of promotion. Both of them have failed to comply with ground rules set for the team. The team manager is more at fault as he has discussed team matters with outside the team employees and has contradicted his own cues. If information churned out from the grapevine turns out to be true, then the organization could lose out on a competent team player. This loss would result in a cascade effect of distrust for the manager, non-cooperation with the new team lead and low team morale.

Solution

It is necessary for smooth team functioning that ground rules for all aspects are co-discussed and strictly implemented. Both a team and its team manager are responsible for maintaining open and constant channels. Indirect cues must never be used as pointers/directives. Everything related to a team in terms of careers, aspirations, plans, meeting, feedback must be discussed in unambiguous terms.

Cross-agendas destroy team cohesiveness. If a team manager interacts with his team in a selective and manipulative manner, he is not respected and looked up to as a role model. Team members also need to be direct about their concerns and queries rather than drawing conclusions based on non-verified cues, only to find out later on that they were being misguided. It is critical that team members do not discuss their development plans with external employees, as this surely adds to the confusion level.

7.2.2 Worksheet for Ground Rules

Ground Rules Conformance

The Ground Rules Conformance worksheet provides a tabular checklist of all requirements and norms that need to be exercised. The responses to which indicate the level of conformance shown by team members under various categories.

Team Member Name: Supporting behavioral traits: Dysfunctional behavioral patterns:			Job Title:	
Standards	Positive Remarks	Negative Comments	Additional Remarks	Action Tools

(Contd...)

Feedback—Overall Rating:				
Fully supports quality improvement feedback				
Gives frank feedback if anyone violates the professional and ethical norms of behavior				
Seeks and gives feedback appropriately and in a timely manner				
Relationships—Overall Rating:				
Supports and encourages others to comply with the team code of ethics				
Respects and appreciates the diversity in the team				
Adapts positively to new or updated ground rules and encourages others to do so				
Presents himself as a role model in building positive relationships				
Shows respect for the expertise and contributions of others				
Applies the right processes and norms in decision-making, communication, conflict resolution				

(Contd...)

Communication—Overall Rating:				
Communicates effectively both verbally and non-verbally				
Maintains and shares accurate and timely documentation and other knowledge reserves				
Demonstrates professional presence in conflict management				
Uses clear and unbiased communication				
Meetings—Overall Rating:				
Attends meetings at the scheduled time and venue				
Participates actively in the discussion				
Shows willingness to reach consensus and respects the meeting agenda				
Whether or not interrupts meetings with side bars				
Self-regulation—Overall Rating:				
Practices fair means				

(Contd...)

Complies with the organizational policies and standard operating procedures under all circumstances				

7.3 Factors for Performance Index—'Leverage Collective Ability'

Not policies and processes,
But self-directed work teams create success
And fuel the wheels of progress.

To enhance a team's maturity level, it is necessary to identify the performance factors and their impact. These factors need to have organizational support in the form of robust policies and systems.

The main factors for raising the performance bar are:

7.3.1 Roles—'Specific and Well Defined'

Clarity of roles and the authority to resolve conflict, when team members do not seem to agree about who does what, is very important to keep things going. The operating principles for each role must be designed in advance, and be linked to the mission statement in clear and concise terms.

Making a team member aware of team's objectives, standards, norms and results expected from each team member, ensures smooth functioning and provides clear role definition, leaving no place for role ambiguity and power vacuums.

7.3.2 Goals—'Be S.M.A.R.T.'

For a team to mature as an integrated unit, specific, measurable, attainable, realistic and deadline-driven goals need to be defined. A sense of timelines keeps a team motivated and constantly on its toes.

Another important factor for creating stable teams is that team members have to be involved while defining the goals and the strategies for achieving them. This is especially true for team goals, where it is critical for a team to have the independence to define them. Too much of organizational control hampers the performance.

Goals are a sure shot way of keeping track of team performance, and deciding whether a team needs re-orientation, if it has lost direction.

7.3.3 Relationships—'Speak a Common Language'

Team relationships need to be fostered and team managers/leaders need to create opportunities for teams to develop the needed levels of trust, cooperation and mutual acceptance.

Team members need ways to resolve problems, and to assure that a good working relationship continues and positive interaction is maintained. Positive relationships greatly contribute to group productivity and morale.

7.3.4 Processes and Policies—'Stability in Productivity'

Horizontal processes pull resources in one direction, whereas the traditional processes pull them in another.

Efficient performance policies and processes are required to remain effective. Again, it is generally a team manager, who can create the time and space for his team to discuss and design its processes, as well as evaluate their effectiveness on a regular basis. Each organization creates the context within which a team functions. The policies, processes and systems of an organization need to be designed in such a way that they provide a major boost to team success.

SDWTs with a standard code of ethics never encounter bitter conflict issues.

7.3.5 Information Reserves—'Value Addition All the Way'

Team members use internal sources of data like functional expertise, domain knowledge, opinions, views, ideas, facts and figures, along with external data, to process it into useful information that can be used to tackle problems. In a way, the ability of a team to collect the data also alters the performance levels.

Proper reporting systems, analyzing tools and communication channels guide in a team's understanding of risks and opportunities. They prepare a team to be in a much better position to take on the competitive challenges.

7.3.6 Task Alignment—'Task Alignment, Efficiency and Effectiveness Go Hand in Hand'

In order to align the tasks with the final mission, there has to be a shared understanding of the task, by analyzing both the high-level implication of the task —> why the task is being undertaken, and also the specific objective —> what goals will be achieved by the task. Team priorities in relation to the tasks need to be in order.

Task alignment is a crucial factor in strengthening established processes in more efficient ways, which in turn leads to an increase in productivity.

7.3.7 Example—'The Communication Mismatch'

Problem Statement

Pat had been promoted from a senior tester to the position of test lead. It had been five months since his promotion and it was time for his first feedback as a team lead. His team manager Phil, was a very good listener, but not a very good documenter. He somehow did not entertain the idea of documenting issues, suggestions and shortfalls, whereas Pat was a good listener and had excellent documentation skills. During the last five months of his role as a test lead, he had noted down certain policy improvements, suggestions to refine the role definitions of the team in his improvement planner. He had discussed the same with Phil informally and was told to discuss them formally in the review meeting.

During the review, Phil did a complete u-turn on his promise about discussing Pat's observations. "Oh common, Pat I must have made an offhand remark, but that does not mean we bring it into a formal meeting. I care for the team much more than you do," said Phil. "But whatever I have to discuss is about team goals, roles and processes. I too want to see our team perform better and that's why I want to discuss my plans with you. We need your support and inputs Phil," replied Pat in a hopeful tone. "Pat, just because I am accommodative, it does not mean you tell me what measures have to be taken to improve performance. I think roles, goals, task alignment, processes, everything is in place and they don't need to be improved as they have been designed by me. Had they not been in place, you would have never got promoted," chided Phil.

Problem Analysis

The main hitch in the problem statement is the lack of managerial support and the tendency of contradictory behavior. Pat tries hard to convince his team manager to have the discussion on fine tuning the performance measures, but the team manager's adamant stand of not entertaining any new ideas wins eventually.

"I think roles, goals, task alignment, processes, everything is in place and they don't need to be improved as they have been designed by me," this statement made by the team manager goes to show that either he is too pompous or he is completely ignorant of the fact that performance measures are not a one-time activity.

Solution

In order to keep team members going, performance measures need to be fine tuned on a regular basis. Roles have to be redrawn when a team undergoes changes. Goals have to be realigned with the organizational goals when organizational changes occur. Team norms and policies have to updated when organizational policies change. Tasks sequencing has to be constantly monitored. Relationships have to be constantly fed with mutual trust. A vigilant team manager is one who appreciates and encourages suggestions for improving performance measures. He along with his team needs to keep the measures up-to-date.

Every team manager along with his team must set clear performance expectations, goals, and measures, by documenting the same for tracking purposes in a performance development plan. A team manager needs to be not only a good listener, but also needs to honor his words. By not doing so, he loses the trust of his team members, and that is a definite sign of unrest within his team.

7.3.8 Worksheets for Improving Performance Index

Relationship Analysis

The Relationship Analysis worksheet provides a clear mechanism to assess the performance gaps arising due to unhealthy relationships, places the involved team members on a performance continuum, and determines the level of improvement or intervention required.

Team Member Name: Describe events when you have exhibited cooperative team spirit even when others were negative and non-cooperative? Describe situations where you were able to strike a win-win scenario? How did you find common ground? What elements of your relationships with others interest you the most, and least? What actions could be taken to improve the current status of relationships? Team Manager's remarks:			
Team Member Name	Positive points of this relationship	Improvement areas in this relationship	Overall value derived from this relationship (1-4 = poor, 5-8 = neutral, 9-12 = good, 12 + excellent)

Team Goals and Roles

The Team Goals and Roles worksheet is a way of making sure that everyone is on the same page of understanding when it comes to team goals and roles.

Goals for the quarter (or a period): Team Name: Goal Statement:			
	January	February	March
Sub Goal # 1	Roles and Responsibilities		
	Actions/Steps required to achieve the objectives		

(Contd...)

	Possible challenges and counter strategies Primary Obstacles and means Secondary Obstacles and means		
	Persons responsible and resources needed		
	Desired outcome		
	Time frame		
Sub Goal # 2	Roles and Responsibilities		
	Actions/Steps required to achieve the objectives		
	Possible challenges and counter strategies Primary Obstacles and means Secondary Obstacles and means		
	Persons responsible and resources needed		
	Desired outcome		
	Time frame		

7.4 Measuring the Outcome—'Narrow the Performance Gaps'

A successful outcome is an amalgamation
Of integrity, consistency and cohesiveness—
Which perpetuates opportunities, boundless.

Progress can be carefully reviewed by using methods like regular meetings, open discussion sessions and progress status reports. Ground rules discussed earlier, make giving and receiving review easier. Performance measurement forms the basis for reward and recognition systems. The various parameters discussed in the earlier section assess how well the SDWT has performed in respect to each one of them.

7.4.1 Types of Performance Measures—'Complete and Comprehensive'

Table 7.1: Types of Performance Measures

Measure	Description
Working Climate	Ratings for the trust levels, integrity and attitudes. Assessment of the motivation levels.
Productivity	Assessment of the work output produced by the team.
Communication	Classification for the level of communication, whether useful or detrimental. Ratings for team communication patterns.
Code of ethics	How well does the group dynamics work in terms of achieving consensus, goal realization, trusting and appreciating each other.
Dynamics	Models for assessing the congruent behavior of the team in several areas like performance and processes. Checklists for pinpointing factors that did well and did not do as expected.
Inputs	Scales for determining how well the team communicates ideas, shares knowledge and enhances each others' skills.
Relationships	How well team members coordinate with each other. Parameters could include the degree of participation in group discussions and team meetings, activities taken up by team members to foster collective growth, how well does the team act as a unit to handle a grave situation. How well do team members take and give feedback.

7.4.2 A Balanced Set—'Again it's all About Teamwork'

The answers to the following four main questions help to reset goals, expectations and team behaviors:

A. How are we performing?

B. What have we achieved so far?

C. What are we required to do next?

D. What support and resources are needed to get to the next level of team maturity?

The definition of performance measures for a specific process and the above questions must involve team members so as to stimulate ideas and reinforce the notion that even performance measurement is teamwork.

When deciding what to measure, start first with measures that track a team rather than individual performance. Check if the measures are balanced and whether the focus caters to several aspects like financial payoff, process compliance, and customer satisfaction. Measures need to also be flexible enough to adapt to team needs. This flexibility encourages team members to perform in accordance with the measures. Team's value-added results, along with measures and performance standards for each result, have to be in concise, specific terms.

Measures are nothing but performance goals that need to be met in order to achieve high performance. The SMART rule holds good for them too. They need to be specific, measurable, achievable, realistic and time-driven. They are the logical link between team resources, activities and outputs.

7.4.3 Formulate Measures—'Four Simple Steps'

Team members need to know how their results are going to impact their organization, for which several performance measures are needed to help them understand the importance of their contribution. An organization needs to know what kind of value and risk they are going to encounter based on these performance indicators.

There are four simple steps for defining the performance measures:

A. Identify all the processes, business objectives and organization goals. In short, spell out what's going to be measured.

B. List out all the tasks and activities needed to achieve the processes, goals and objectives.

C. Develop the performance measures. Two types of performance measures come into play. First type is milestones/deadlines which let you know how close you are to meeting the objectives and second type is checkpoints/drivers which let you know whether your current tasks and activities are robust enough to let you achieve the processes, objectives and goals.

D. The type of measurement needs to be defined, whether it is a plain numeric rating or a descriptive response. For example, in the case of processes, a team can design something called as a process map, where the transformation process, right from inputs to outputs and activities in between are tracked for any team-related process—for example, product development.

7.4.4 Rewards and Recognition—'Alignment with Results'

Top management must ensure that their systems of rewards and recognition are carefully aligned with strategic and operational goals. Validated measures and metrics provide opportunities to recognize and reward good performance.

Though technically speaking rewards and recognition is a separate process, but in conjunction with the performance measurement, the following aspects of the rewards and recognition system need to be addressed:

1. Budgetary requirements for rewards.
2. Types of rewards—gift certificates, cash awards, certificate of merit, stock options, bonus.
3. Eligibility criteria.
4. Improvement plans.

Performance does impact compensation. As I mentioned earlier that profit sharing is more popular than any other form of reward system.

Just as the performance system affects the rewards and recognition process, similarly the quality of recognition policies impact team performance too.

7.4.5 360-Degrees Evaluation—'Honest and Objective Feedback'

In a typical 360 degrees system, a teammate chooses other team members for evaluation. The number ranges between five and ten. The team member then fills out a questionnaire or a form-based survey, and rates the chosen team members based on several parameters and ratings. Each team member participates separately in the evaluation process, and it would be best to keep individual team member's participation anonymous. Anonymity ensures objective and honest responses. All the results are collected, tabulated, and then discussed with their team manager to work out improvement plans for each of the team members assessed. He then discusses all the findings with the concerned team members without disclosing the identity of the assessor. This kind of overall ranking system gives a foolproof status of performance levels, and hence a more effective way for finding the best possible solutions.

7.4.6 Scenario Testing—'Careful Analysis'

Scenario testing is a very effective method for measuring the outcome. A team is supposed to rate the performance based on various aspects like level of cooperation, level of trust or any of the performance factors mentioned earlier. The responses are captured through a comprehensive questionnaire. Mostly this questionnaire has rating-based responses or team members can also provide concise answers. These responses are then studied and tabulated on the basis of criteria in terms of low to high priority and importance. The post-scenario questionnaire can also incorporate questions about the extent to which the simulation environment seemed to be consistent with what could actually occur in the physical operational setup. Scenario testing minimizes the risks of unexpected surprises, and can be used to assess various alternatives as well as their impact on goals.

Team performance evaluation and the reorientation training are key factors related to the successfulness of SDWTs in organizations.

7.4.7 Worksheets for Measuring the Outcome

Performance Appraisal

The Performance Appraisal worksheet brings about effective job performance, establishes future goals and responsibilities, and increases professional growth, based on the gaps and the overall rating assigned.

Team Member Name: Monitoring comments:					
Goal/Responsibility (Related to inputs, relationships, communication, productivity, etc.)	Results	Evidence to support results	Specific examples	Below performance level—Causes and action tools	Overall rating
#1					
#2					
#3					
#4					
Additional competencies acquired (skills, domain knowledge): Development goals (training, additional roles, competencies, etc.) for the next reporting period: Extrinsic and intrinsic consequences: Development areas outside of job domain:					

Performance Problem Analysis

The Performance Problem Analysis worksheet captures details about a performance problem, which can be filled by a team manager in collaboration with his team members. It is a means of obtaining critical information, which then is used to re-draw the road map for overcoming the performance discrepancies.

Performance Reporting Period:
1. Name of the Team Member:
2. Job Title and responsibilities:
3. Details of the areas of performance dissatisfaction:
4. What are the expectations from team member:
5. What is he actually doing:
6. Analysis of the gap in terms of time, money and efforts:
7. Analysis of the consequences both real and perceived:
8. Is closing the gaps justifiable:
9. Analysis of external factors that may be causing performance problems (ground rules, managerial inputs, motivation, accountability, rewards, etc.):

(Contd...)

10. What can be done to close the gaps:
    (a) Training
    (b) Support procedures
    (c) Required skills
11. Classification of performance issues:
    (a) Urgent
    (b) Medium
    (c) Can be attended in due course
12. Probable consequences if the solutions fail:
13. Possible solutions:
14. Best solution and Rationale:
15. Implementation details and follow-up guidelines:

Discuss and enlist points related to the appraisee's career direction options: (to be filled based on the above responses and the information gathered from the performance appraisal worksheet)

Performance-Oriented Team

The Performance-oriented Team worksheet pinpoints areas in which the SDWT as a whole fails to perform and excels too.

Team Name:

Team Manager's Name:

Additional remarks of the Team Manager:

Rate on scale of 1-10: 1=this is not valid at all and 10=this is valid most of the time

or

Rate on the basis of frequency of meeting a particular success criteria, the ratings can be classified as 1=Not at all, 2=Rarely, 3=Sometimes, 4=Most often, and 5=Always

Main Category—Team Environment

Sub-Category	Rating
Is the mission of the team readily comprehended and carried out	
Are the work patterns and processes well described and employed	
Are the roles and responsibilities interpreted correctly	

(Contd...)

Is there any role overlap	
Is ownership shared and willingly adhered to	
Do team members give and receive feedback without inhibitions	
Does the team have a strong identity	
Are organizational support structures and executive sponsorship available	
Is the team focused and customer centric	
Main Category—Team Processes	
Sub-Category	Rating
Is intelligent risk taken	
Is problem-solving process in place	
Are communication guidelines in place	
Are meeting ground rules defined and followed	
Are there adequate measures and tools for performance measurement and reporting	
Are team members given a chance to work on challenging tasks and stretch their knowledge and capabilities	
Is there a provision for ongoing evaluation and action planning	
Is the team keen on regular training and development sessions	
Main Category—Team Members	
Sub-Category	Rating
Are team members honest with each other and the team mission	
Do they motivate each other	
Do they appreciate and acknowledge each other's success	
Do they receive non-threatening and honest feedback from their colleagues	
Is there a strong alignment between team members	

(Contd…)

Do they take collective ownership even for below the mark results	
Do they give each other space and equal opportunity to develop, both personally and professionally	
Do they make positive contributions and help the team achieve objectives	
Are team members aligned to a common future	
Do they leverage each other's strengths	
Inputs from team members (this helps to decide whether or not problems in the performance management system itself are the main cause of low team performance) Assessment of the overall performance system: Are the performance system and pay integrated (Yes/No) If no, then what is the proposed action: How integral the performance system is to the self-appraisal process (high, medium, low) If low, then what is the proposed action: Do team members have a clear definition of their performance baselines, goals, results, pay and rewards criteria, indicators (Yes/No/Partly) If no and partly, then what is the proposed action: Is sufficient time and resources allocated to performance management (Yes/No/Partly) If no and partly, then what is the proposed action:	

7.5 Team Feedback—'Performance for Reorientation'

Specific feedback
Reinforces performance,
Helps to rise above industry benchmark
And enhances team conformance.

When feedback becomes a collaborative effort, then team members *intuitively* agree to the performance loop and give their full commitment to it. SDWTs learn from the feedback they receive based on their output. This feedback data needs to be collected, analyzed, evaluated and tabulated so that it can be used as an input for forming new ground rules or altering existing ones. Feedback has to be delivered judiciously and frequently. To be effective, performance assessment must be objective and fair.

Constant review and checkpoints allow both teams and organizations to correct discrepancies in existing practices and systems, and eliminate the ineffective ones. Another important aspect of performance feedback is that it sets up a link between collaborative efforts and team success.

Reorientation is about establishing goals, measuring current level of performance to measure the gap between the current and expected level, and then planning, implementing and monitoring strategies in order to overcome the shortfalls. A plan to collect and summarize the data so that a team knows how it is performing compared to the performance benchmark has a big payoff. Skills to analyze the performance data are needed to remodel the data into logical information.

7.5.1 Feedback Framework—'Greater Operational Efficiency'

A. Planning

Considerable amount of time is required for planning how the feedback will be fed back into the system, to bring about the required improvements. It can either be presented in a graphical format or an elaborate report—factor-wise can be generated on a weekly basis and then collated at the end of every month. A team manager may send out a brief summary of the feedback agenda prior to each review meeting. Specific and tangible examples and experiences need to be cited in order to get the feedback across correctly.

Team members need to be given sufficient time to prepare themselves for the feedback. They could be given a questionnaire to fill up before attending the meeting. The questionnaire can have questions related to individual evaluation of performance in terms of accomplishments, goals for the next performance reporting period and the gaps detected.

B. Tone of the Feedback Process

Any feedback has two sides—positive and critical, but it is the duty of each and every team manager to present both the aspects in an encouraging manner. The positive achievements need to be appreciated and rewarded, whereas the negative feedback must not be used as a means of playing politics. If negative feedback is shared by employing motivational ways then this is bound to lift the employee morale, which in turn facilitates a team to overcome the negative points. A team manager should always present the positive experiences first, and also while ending the review meeting he can make use of motivating words.

C. Two Way Feedback

Feedback is both about giving and receiving. Team members are entitled to equal opportunity to share their views and suggestions about the various factors including the feedback loop. It is quite possible that team members can present valid points or action items, which the management may have overlooked all this while.

D. New Direction

While discussing future goals, team members need to keep the criticism positive, which allows them to focus on goal definition rather than team members who have caused low performance. New direction is not about comparing one employee with the other. Once the future goals have been identified for a team as well as individuals, a team manager needs to show them how important these goals are for their organization—*the big picture* is what the feedback loop is all about eventually.

E. Post Feedback Checkpoints

Feedback is not only about discussing improvement areas but also about drawing out action plans for the same. The deadlines and the follow up schedule also need to be discussed in detail.

The golden rule of feedback is that it is always to be shared in concrete terms and not by making generic remarks. For example, a particular team manager could say something like the team has done a great job by delivering a bug-free product two days before the deadline, rather than just putting in a casual statement like well done team. Specific examples reinforce performance.

Feedback resets inappropriate ground rules by addressing the following questions:

1. What have been the major team accomplishments?
2. What new skills have been acquired by the team?
3. What insights have been gained?
4. Which risks have been and have not been nullified?
5. What are the improvements areas?
6. What lessons have been learned?

7.5.2 Example—'A Sidelined Star'

Problem Statement

Nick—marketing executive walked over to his colleague's workstation to share his frustration. "You seem to be upset. What's the matter?," inquired his colleague. "Yes a lot, my self-image is totally shattered. How would one feel after being ripped apart at the performance review session? Not once, did my team manager tell me anything negative about my performance during the last review period of six months. Today, he rates my performance as below average. With due respect to everyone on the team, you and the rest know what my performance level is like?" "Yea... It's a 10+," affirmed his colleague with a thumbs-up sign. "What about the performance plan?," asked his colleague. "He did not bother to look at it even once during those 30 minutes of review. He never gave me a chance to defend myself. I really don't know what do to."

Problem Analysis

Nick's team manager does not seem to believe in constant feedback and regular overhauls. He somehow seems to fear good performance and also fails to appreciate the same. At the same time, he justifies his fear by demeaning good performance during the performance review meetings. And this is what exactly the team manager has done during Nick's review. In order to cover up his own flaw of not keeping a regular check on the performance of his team, he devalues the results given by a competent team member.

Nick's self-esteem is at an all-time low, in spite of meeting the performance standards, he is reprimanded. He is clueless as to how he is going to handle this unfair treatment.

Solution

The team manager needs to be trained in the performance management process in order to overcome his faulty behavioral pattern. He needs to reinforce the newly learned skills, by acknowledging good performance through formal and informal ways, and at the same time pinpoint any pitfalls in an encouraging tone.

It is essential for the team manager to discuss the performance improvement plans with his team. Feedback has to be two-way, and both team members and their team manager need to work on the areas needed to be measured, performance standards, improvement plans and future goals.

To set higher levels of performance, mutual agreement is very crucial. And any agreement can be reached only when there is a two-way exchange of clear communication. Just as every team manager prepares a report of observations, suggestions, appreciation and improvement points, so do his team members prepare a report stating the same and exchange their details. Based on this mutual feedback, necessary adjustment can be made in the performance improvement plans and everyone gets to benefit from the same, due to which good performance is neither reprimanded nor ignored.

7.5.3 Worksheet for Team Feedback

Team Feedback Results

The Team Feedback Results worksheet rates each team member based on various aspects. Here there are three ratings taken into consideration—self, others and team manager. At the same time, team member's inputs on the overall team performance are also solicited.

Team Member Name: Rate each team member: Overall Rating (1-5) 1-lowest; 5-highest				
Feedback aspect	Rating by self	Rating by others	Rating by team manager	Comments
Personal Task Orientation:				
Detail-oriented				
Highly motivated				
Consistently takes initiative				
Risk taking attitude				
Group Task Orientation:				
Strives hard to maintain the group identity				
Makes tough calls for the group				
Stands by the group through thick and thin				
Social Orientation:				
Respects diversity				
Genuinely cares for others' needs				
Balances and complements team members				
Builds strong partnerships with client				

(Contd…)

1 – Successful, 2 – Partially, 3 – Unsuccessful
How successful has the team been in moving toward its mission:
How successful has the team been in facing challenges:
Is everyone on the team contributing substantially:
Is everyone practising team guidelines, norms and values:

7.5.4 *Advantages of the Performance Maturity Loop*

A. The quality of interaction among team members can be judged and provisions to fill in the vacuums can be designed.

B. Group rationalization is a key benefit as it motivates team members to identify and deprecate false assumptions that they had made in the past, which affected their performance adversely.

C. The performance maturity loop is a fact-based approach to performance enhancement.

D. Performance assessment presents a clear picture of a team's progress level, which enables a team to take the right amount of risks.

E. Encourages dissension against extreme and irrational stereotypes. This ensures that the performance loopholes caused by irrational and extreme views and standpoints are corrected.

F. Past performance, future potential and competencies of a team can be evaluated and corrected to close the gaps.

G. Training needs can be plotted out with a proper strategy in place for the same.

H. One can evaluate the extent to which goals are clear and unambiguous. The degree of ownership can be measured to correct any inequalities in responsibility assignment.

7.6 Chapter Recap

1. Firmly ingrained ground rules are values and guidelines governing a team's expectations of acceptable behavior. Ground rules are necessary to

voice disagreements and conflicts, in a positive, healthy manner.

2. Well defined roles, S.M.A.R.T. goals, healthy relationships, stable processes, information reserves and logical task alignment are critical factors for team performance.
3. Performance measurement forms the basis for reward and recognition systems, and is developed using several measures, right from working climate to team member relationships.
4. A good feedback is one which gives team members an opportunity to learn about themselves and how they interact with each other. It helps them to focus more on future direction than past performance.

PART III

From Action to More Action: The Transformation Continues

8

Energy-Sharing Paradigm—'Build a Global Intelligence Network'

The whole truly
Is greater than the sum of its parts
As all conflicts it thwarts.

Most people are comfortable with the concept that "Two heads are better than one", but what about the practical aspect, it is here that the Energy-Sharing Paradigm or simply put 'Believe that everyone has something to share' comes into play.

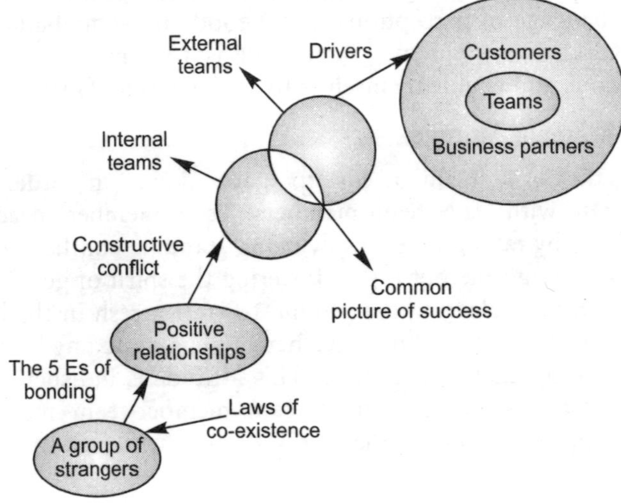

Fig. 8.1: The Energy-sharing Paradigm

Creating stable team dynamics within a group of diverse people is a significant challenge in today's workplace. The Energy-Sharing Paradigm definitely eases up the process and makes it more enjoyable. Many studies have shown that diversity in human energy actually leads to increased creativity. Research has also shown that the failure to successfully integrate diverse workforces has negative impact on the organizational performance. The laws of co-existence, positive team relationships and proper conflict management, aid team members to focus their attention on optimal performance using their diverse energy capital.

8.1 The Laws of Co-existence—'Turn Weak Areas into Strengths'

Co-existence is not a choice
But a necessity
That leads to team rejoice.

Teams must always strive to create an environment that is friendly and motivating. Diversity in ideas and opinions certainly needs to be encouraged.

A. Removal of Hindering Perceptions

People who board the team band wagon come with a unique baggage of perceptions, some good and some bad. The role of a team as an integrated unit is to remove the bad perceptions and enable themselves to succeed as an SDWT.

B. Slow Down Attitude

At times, a team needs to pace down in order to collaborate with other team members. Team members need to realize that by taking time to solve long-standing conflicts, they are not wasting time but rather fostering the spirit of goodwill. In fact, they are clearing the ground to start afresh in the best possible way. They need to strive hard to eliminate any kind of cynicism and negative exchange. This attitude is indispensable in all situations, whether it is team member-team member relationships or with team managers, or even with customers.

C. Teams are a Family

SDWTs are more than just functional units operating out of office space in a typical co-worker environment. They need to relate to each other just like members of a family do, even if they are in the work setup. They need to care for each other, trust each other and nurture each other's dreams, just the way each one of us here do for our blood relations. In short, team members are needed to care about each other, both professionally and personally. In tandem, team managers also need to put in efforts to keep the family united.

D. Cordial Relations all the Way

At times, the most innovative ideas stem from informal interactions outside of the office. Highly energetic teams maintain harmonious relationships not just at work, but also continue to interact with each other with the same level of harmony, even in the outside environment.

E. Trust Givers

It is always good to have at least two to three trust givers. Their actions and behavior are in sync, which gives others the confidence to move along the same course. Naturally, the integrity of the whole team tends to rise.

F. Emotional Literacy

Apart from the regular training, induction and orientation sessions, the management needs to conduct well-being sessions. These programs are aimed at developing the social aspect of team interaction rather than technical skills. These social development sessions are meant to improve relationships.

G. Peer Support

A 'no-blame' system is the best way to resolve disruptive procedures and behaviors. Everyone on a team must agree that sharing concerns and ideas is a great learning experience, and respect for everyone's views works wonders. Peer support sets a positive context for working with others to generate solutions.

H. The PAL Formula

Patience, adjustment and loyalty are the key ingredients that forge strong emotional cords. Emotional connections eliminate obstacles caused by unfair professional desires. With PAL, people realize that by playing politics or sidestepping others, a team is not going to perform at all.

Co-existence and conformity is possible, when team members choose to go along with the views of others on a team. The above laws are nothing but periodic tune-ups for keeping every team on the track of group thinking mentality.

8.1.1 Example—'The Insecure Team Manager'

Problem Statement

During a one-one session with his team manager, Tim put across a valid point. "Sir, I think we need to streamline the work reporting tool as it is taking up a lot of time of the team. The tool needs some fine tuning," Tim said assertively. "Well, let me remind you Tim that I am the boss here, and I am the one who decides what's good and what's not good for the team," replied the team manager sternly. "Sir it's just not me but the entire team feels so." "Oh, so now you are garnering support from the others to put me down. Look Tim, you can't play games with me and remember your appraisal is in my hands," threatened the team manager.

Tim walked out of the cabin in dilemma—whether it will be better to drop the topic or have a word with his team manager one more time.

Problem Analysis

A team manager's distrust and suspicious attitude is the main hindrance for a team's progress, as he considers any improvement tips or suggestions, a threat to his position.

In the above example, the team manager's threatening tone discourages the team from coming up with innovative ideas and solutions, as they know that they are never going to get the required executive sponsorship. Moreover, their career is at stake as all the performance reports and appraisal ratings will be affected negatively, if they were to become aggressive in their approach towards their team manager.

By discouraging one employee, the team manager is discouraging the rest of the team. At the same time, his threatening tone causes discomfort in the team. Even if there is one bold team member who wants to put up his suggestions, the rest of the team considers him as a roadblock because their performance rating could be affected negatively.

Solution

Co-existence is the key to team performance. Only when a team and its team manager exchange views and opinions will both of them benefit from the same. The team manager must not view bright suggestions and policy changes as a threat to his position, rather it is his duty to show commitment to the development of the diversity that his team brings with it. Instead of fearing it, if he encourages his team, then this not only leads to an increase in his personal pride but also strengthens the bonds of co-existence.

Empathetic listening is not a choice but a necessity for any team manager to be facilitative. By turning full attention to team members, the team manager realizes that his suspicion of team members trying to usurp his position is totally baseless. He realizes that rather by not hearing out his team members' ideas, he would have experienced a big loss in terms of performance improvement.

It is top management's responsibility to orient each team manager, by giving him the required training to create an environment, where each team member feels totally free to express an idea or concern.

8.2 Positive Team Relationships—'Create a Motivating Setup'

Valuing each other is the basis
Of healthy relationships in a self-driven team
Which creates dynamics, supreme.

What is an organization's goal? A dream-team, right! And how can it achieve this goal...yes, of course through positive team relationships. Well, think about it. You as the team manager of a team need the cooperation of your team in order to successfully meet the milestones. Without your team, you truly can never ever be able to achieve your dream. The bottom-line is you need them to "get on board" and perform as a stable, strong, integrated unit.

Positive, supportive relationships at workplace produce the best ideas. The most effective decisions are made from the bottom up. The challenge for an SDWT is to find the unique combination of values that a team relates to and that which meet individual needs so that each team member is motivated to accept the value system for the good of the entire team.

Here are the keys to building positive team linkages, *the 5 Es of team bonding:*

A. Empathetic Attitude

Empathy is an extremely important team concept. Good listening skills are necessary in order to succeed in stabilizing good relationships and ensuring that each person is entitled to equal talk time.

B. Endeavor to Communicate

'Working together' is about communicating and accepting each other's identity. None of the team members in a team can afford to be timid or inactive in terms of contributing through discussions, informal meetings and brainstorming sessions. This includes responding to each other's messages, queries, requests and suggestions in a timely fashion. Team members must learn to take any critical remark in the positive sense. Viewing criticism as an opportunity for improvement affects team throughput positively.

C. Eliminate Egos Through Self-Analysis

Each team member needs to indulge in some amount of introspection. Examining one's own behavior to be sure that one is not anchoring irrational dispositions or supporting team members with such stands, helps to set things in order. Each team member needs to foster positive attitude within and also surround himself with positive people.

Team members need to look for non-verbal cues, to analyze their own behavior, to confirm whether there is any faulty pattern in their reactions that needs to be changed. Observing other team members' reactions also lets one reorient oneself. This self-adjusting attitude ensures that team members look at each conflicting situation as a source of learning opportunity, and not as a personal threat.

D. Equal Access to Knowledge

For everyone to be on the same level of understanding, knowledge and information has to be accessible to one and all. In the real world, due to competitive factors, some people have unlimited access, while the rest are not even allowed 25 per cent of the access. For example, in a team if person A is not told about the new calculation rules just because he is too competent and others fear that he can supersede them, then they will misuse this opportunity to jeopardize his career by withholding the information updates. Unaware of the new calculation rules, he will continue working on the outdated rules, thereby affecting his output and reward in turn. This is a sure shot trigger for unrest in a team. Therefore, it is very critical to ensure that the required information within the legal confines gets disseminated at the appropriate time and in technically correct terms. It is always best to share as much as possible, and as soon as possible.

E. Evenhanded Representation in the Value System

Team values are beliefs that are important to all team members. These values come into play each time team members communicate with each other, and they are the source of rich discussions and constructive conflicts.

Each team member brings a unique value system to the table. One way of unifying a team is to instill common values, by asking teammates what is important to them and then compiling their responses. This list is an input to building team values based on the common and most important values in relation to an organization.

8.2.1 Example—'The Disoriented Delegate'

Problem Statement

In the absence of the team manager, Jim, a senior team leader had been asked to conduct the weekly status update meeting. The team manager had discussed with him in detail as to what action items needed to be worked on and what updates needed to be shared with the team.

After the meeting was over, the rest of the team seemed dissatisfied with how the session was conducted by Jim. "He is so much unlike our team manager. He gave us each only a minute to discuss last week's progress," said Ken, a programmer analyst. "I just hope that our team manager gets back soon. There is no point in attending meetings where we are not allowed to speak or discuss. Here we are worried about the upcoming delivery and Jim was more concerned with the annual gathering," added Clara, a tester. "He didn't even bother to discuss the problem areas and update us with the latest customer inputs. Really don't know how I am going to complete my database package without the latest updates," said a frustrated database analyst, Stella.

Problem Analysis

From the negative reactions of the team, it is obvious that their temporary team manager Jim is not aware of the *5 Es* and simply does not believe in sharing space with his colleagues. Due to his inefficiency, team members are clueless about the following week's action items. He has not shared valuable updates/knowledge reserves that have been passed to him by the team manager. Unequal access to knowledge reserves is something that is definitely going to affect the delivery timelines and the client trust levels.

Jim does not seem to share the team values as the other team members share. During the meeting, instead of worrying about the delivery deadlines, he is more interested in talking about the annual gathering.

Solution

The team needs to report Jim's lack of support to their team manager. Their team manager then needs to discuss the issue with Jim and draw out an improvement plan, where he needs to be mentored to imbibe good communication and interpersonal skills. He could also be sent to a personality development workshop, where he gets to learn the techniques of empathy and trust.

To teach Jim a lesson, the team manager could attribute the failure to meet deadlines to Jim's disoriented focus. This way, Jim will come to learn that by not sharing common team values, he has to bear the brunt of failure.

Another simple trick is that the team manager could conduct a meeting where all team members except Jim are given equal talk time. By the end of the meeting, Jim will realize his mistakes, and understand the importance of equal freedom and flexibility. He will understand and appreciate the importance of empathetic mentoring.

8.2.2 Worksheet for Positive Team Relationships

The Level of Positive Relationships

The Level of Positive Relationships worksheet identifies team members who play an important role in forging positive bonds in the SDWT.

Team Member Name: Team Manager's Comments:	
Categories	Rating/Remarks
Communication:	
Is the team member a good communicator	
What is the level of assertiveness	
Is the team member a good listener	
What is the level of interaction	
What is the response promptness level	
Vision for the team:	
Does the team member think long-term	
Is the team member close to the team values	
Does the team member	

(Contd...)

support positive change	
Is the team member able to prioritize	
Team Player:	
Is the team member trusted	
Is the team member responsible	
Does the team member follow ground rules	
Does the team member motivate colleagues	
Level of willingness to take tough calls	
Knowledge Sharing:	
Does the team member respond to work-related queries	
Does the team member share important updates	
Does the team member show initiative to keep other team members informed	
Does the team member have cross-agendas and hides information	
People Skills:	
Does the team member have a self-adjusting attitude	
What is the level of willingness to pitch in to help others	
Does the team member have good manners	

(Contd...)

Is the team member able to exercise a positive influence on the way others think and act	
Does the team member work with others as an integrated unit or as a lone performer	

8.3 Constructive Conflict—'Diffuse Adversity'

Conflicts need to be managed properly
In order to leverage the diversity
And diffuse the adversity.

Professionals today must work closely with more people than ever before. When expectations are not met, team members tend to be frustrated or even angry, and this results in clashes. Research shows that 18 per cent of a team manager's time, i.e., more than nine weeks out of every year is spent resolving clashes among employees. The following aspects minimize the chances of negative conflicts.

A. Driving Factors and Restraining Factors

In order for the SDWT to give in its best, it needs to separate out the driving factors from the obstacles when it comes to conflict resolution. Driving factors lead to positive conflict, and assist team members in reaching a solution. The obstacles or the restraining factors are aspects that keep a team from finding a resolution. Once both types of factors are categorized, they need to be ranked. The restraining factors that are easiest to tackle need to be tackled first, whereas in the case of driving factors, the strongest one needs to be handled first.

B. Willingness to Work in Synergy

Collaboration is about proactive action and reaction. There are two main types of behaviors involved in collaboration—Relationship and task behaviors. Relationship behaviors are related to the interpersonal dynamics, whereas tasks behaviors are concerned with actions related to the mission and objectives. The collaborative mode needs to be 'on' in both the scenarios. A well-balanced mix of these two aspects lets a team perform in a smooth fashion.

This mix enables a team to develop interpersonal relationships in such a way that this in turn boosts the tasks relationships.

If each team member is equally valued for his feedback, then the entire team can gain valuable learning experiences from the feedback responses. This learning can then be applied to their tasks to achieve better performance.

C. Corporate Social Responsibility

We all have a personal responsibility to each other. The same holds true for teams as they are responsible for bringing about a positive change in business. Just as we have our individual ethics, similarly each SDWT needs to operate within the confines of business ethics. At the end of the day, an organization is about brand building, and one of the most important factors for this is its teams. Organizations have to maintain their unique sales proposition by juggling a mix of internal as well as external factors. External factors include government regulations, competition, price pressures, etc. On the internal front, the most crucial aspect is teams who show a high degree of corporate responsibility.

D. Developing Commitment

One of the most effective ways of avoiding conflict is to capitalize on the factors that are mutually important to team members. Working on these mutually beneficial aspects surely fosters positive relationships. To get people committed to the project, one needs to find out what motivates them the best. The facilitators have to understand and implement provisions catering to the points mentioned as follows:

1. Team members need to know what is expected of them.
2. The benefits they will receive.
3. And what rewards they will receive.

E. Willingness to Deal with Conflict

Conflict is part of living; it is neither good nor bad. The challenge is to be willing to make conflict constructive. The main underlying factor for dealing with conflict is that of the willingness to resolve it. There are two viewpoints to this. Some team members know how to work out the solution but are not willing to do so, while the rest may be willing but do not have the right conflict handling skills. Training and counseling cut down the waves of resistance, and make people more capable and willing to reach a consensus.

The most important norms as regards to willingness to deal with conflict are how team decisions are taken and how disagreements are dealt with. These norms are frames of reference that provide new options for team dialogue and ways of working in unison.

8.3.1 Example—'Mixed Signals'

Problem Statement

Lynn, a technical consultant and Fiona her colleague were chatting over coffee. "Well, I really can't adjust with James and his ways," complained Lynn. "Why do you say so?", asked Fiona. "Well, the other day James had given me an appointment and I went over to him at the fixed time. I was supposed to present my new idea to him. I was really excited as he showed interest, but then when I went to meet him, he really didn't seem to be interested," continued Lynn. "What happened?" inquired Fiona. "First he kept me waiting as he had to complete a report, then another ten minutes he was on the phone. Finally, after twenty minutes or so, he asked me to continue, but even before I began I could sense his restlessness. He was fidgeting with his mobile, playing around with the paper weight and rolling his eyes. Barely had five minutes passed and he said he will reschedule the meeting," said Lynn in an exasperated tone.

Problem Analysis

James appears to be a bag of mixed signals. His initial interest in the new idea and then the sudden transformation into rolling eyes, fidgeting hands and careless attitude, are bound to make Lynn angry. At the same time, Lynn's abrupt conclusion of his not being cooperative is not fully justifiable. She should approach him one more time to find the true reason for his behavior. James has definitely failed in playing the role of a good communicator, which involves both focused talking and attentive listening.

Solution

Body language plays a crucial role in identifying the nature of conflicts. While communicating team members have to be careful about their body language and non-verbal cues. They need to ensure that their actions and non-verbal cues are in sync to avoid sending out mixed signals.

It is of utmost importance to properly organize all types of team communication in order to keep distractions at bay.

Explicitly set forth ground rules for decision-making, discussion, brainstorming and meetings need to be designed and strictly adhered to. Ground rules ensure that team members do not waste time by shifting the agenda of the meeting/discussion to suit their own personal needs and moods. This increases the willingness to deal with any conflict as everyone is on the same page of understanding.

8.3.2 Worksheets for Constructive Conflicts

Conflict Analysis

The responses collated from the Conflict Analysis worksheet gauges the willingness level of team members to solve conflicts constructively, thereby enabling the SDWT to focus on the behaviors and conflict, and not on the people involved.

Team Member Name: Team Manager's conclusion on the personality type:		
Item	Description	Team Manager's remarks
Team member's interests and priorities	Constructive/destructive	Accepted/Rejected/ Escalated Appropriate conflict resolution strategy

(Contd...)

Aspects of other team members that you disagree with and how would you like to change them		
Preconceived notions and shared interests		
Level of willingness to resolve the conflict	Sample response 4 where 4 is a rating on a 1-5 scale 1 being non-willing and 5 being extremely willing	

Conflict Resolution Form

The Conflict Resolution form identifies conflicts before they turn into destructive ones. This in turn creates a better working environment that attracts and retains employees.

Reporting Team Member:
Conflict # 1
Nature and history of conflict:
Last Resolution of conflict (if any):
Status: Open/Resolved:
Team Members involved:
List two things that you could have done differently to avoid conflict:
What would you like to say to the team members involved in this conflict:
Any other references/points of contact from whom additional information about the conflict can be acquired:
New proposed Resolution and date (if still open):
Escalation required:

8.4 Energizing Every Unit—'From I Win to We Win'

Value team members for who they are,
Value team members for what they are,
Only then organizations become a corporate star.

Engaging with each other and creating a common picture of success is the ultimate goal of an SDWT, and eventually of an organization. What makes any team perform? The answer is 'Intelligent Energy'. The motivational power of human factors comes from meeting the intellectual and emotional needs of people. Intelligent energy can be fed and nurtured through the SCS drivers—**Security, Challenges** and **Sense of Growth.** With these support systems in place, enormous productive energy can be created.

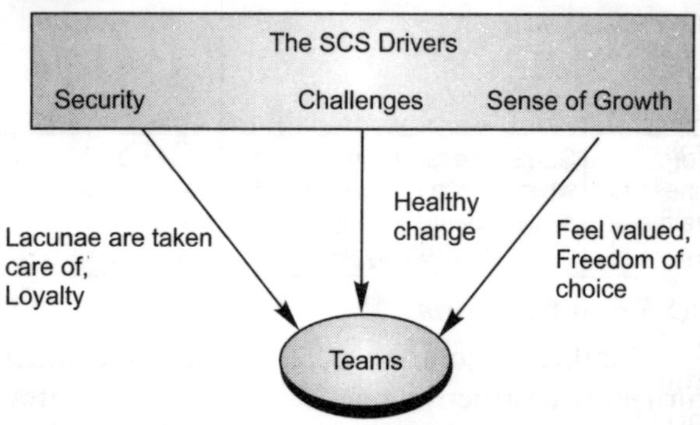

Fig. 8.2: The SCS Drivers

A. Challenges

Providing challenging goals at regular intervals is something that ambitious team members thrive on. Any challenge which brings about a healthy change is welcomed with open arms by a team.

When teams are presented with stimulating challenges, they tend to work together and pool their skills to overcome the impossible. When positive changes occur, both the management and teams feel effective, and the staff retention improves. Realistically set challenges can be used to inspire team members to do something extraordinary. Teams tend to learn more when their mental limits are challenged.

B. Security

Many people look great on paper, but in the real world they fail. This does not mean that they are good for nothing; every organization needs to assure team members that they will be trained and honed to fit the bill. For example, it is quite possible that a certain team member could have been selected purely on the basis of his flawless communication skills, but needs appropriate training to perform the designated role. Here, the management can provide him the necessary training and at the same time leverage his positive traits. This goes to show that the organization values his skills and career security, and also is ready to invest in helping him to overcome his gaps. Research shows that employees are more productive and loyal when they don't have to worry about layoffs or downsizing.

Effective team managers maintain this sense of security by regularly communicating relevant developments to their team members. They do not keep a team in the dark, especially in case of issues that impact employees directly.

C. Sense of Growth

Sense of growth involves two aspects—freedom to choose and a sense of feeling valued. Team members need to have several choices to choose from, they need to be given an opportunity to express their concerns and hopes so that appropriate choices can be designed by a team. The choice of making a level-headed decision ensures a confirmed buy-in from team members, which in turn makes them feel valued for their individuality. In order to retain valuable human resources, the management needs to understand the growth and enhancement needs of team members, and work on the same too.

Mismanagement of energy occurs when team members are over-utilized and feel that their energy cannot match up to the capacity or overload, something we all know as *burnout*. At any given point in time, a team manager needs to ensure that while fueling the generator of intelligent energy, burnout is not permissible.

8.5 Chapter Recap

1. Laws of coexistence create the right dynamics that eventually lead to healthy, resilient and productive working patterns, and collaborative relationships.
2. What makes an SDWT tick? Positive relationships are the most important driver in delivering team success. The most successful teams are those who understand themselves as well as others, can relate and adapt

to the needs of a situation, and communicate their understanding of it well. They also believe in sharing intelligent energy—knowledge and unique values for the betterment of teams (The 5 Es).

3. Differences cannot be avoided, but rather they can be dealt with prudence to derive positive outcomes. Constructive conflict leads to productive solutions, exposes key issues and stimulates critical thinking.
4. The SCS drivers—Security, Challenges and Sense of Growth are important for fueling the emotional energy and knowledge that motivate a group of individuals to perform as a well-connected team.

9

Accountability is the Name of the Game—'The Main Pillar of Self-led Teamwork'

Every employee counts,
Every SDWT counts,
With which all problems
An organization surmounts.

The competitive landscape is not only about globalization, but also includes the human landscape—the soft side of business. This is where accountability and de-layering of power comes into play. Accountability and devolvement ensures that inadequate performers feel pressurized to perform.

9.1 Mutual Enrichment—'Positive Psychology'

Create an environment
Where team members
Can count on each other
To alleviate emotional embers.

'Clarity + Buy-in + Trust – Ambiguity = Accountability'

Accountability is the difference between "What makes team members work?" and "What makes them perform well?" By placing the onus on the SDWT for developing improvement plans and putting them in action is a sure fire way of enabling collective performance. This is what I call 'Mutual Enrichment'.

An environment where team members are able to explain to each other their actions and consequences, without indulging in personal biases and back biting, is the key to accountability. This is where high trust levels play a major role for creating the much needed buy-in on various aspects like role clarity, goal clarity and purpose clarity. Clarity is essential for creating clear-cut ownership boundaries.

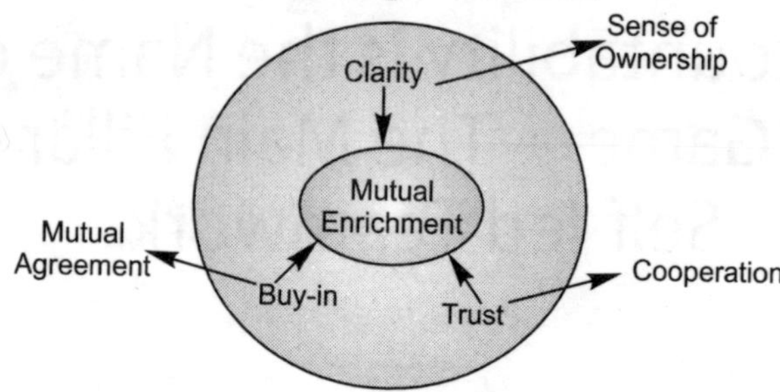

Fig. 9.1: Mutual Enrichment

The above elements provide a helping hand to team members in getting rid of faulty interpersonal relationships. They no longer justify their contributions out of sheer guilt. Trust allows people to own up for their results without taking on a defensive stand. Clarity prevents team members from constantly explaining each and every action of theirs. Team players accept not only individual accountability and take full responsibility to complete their own assignments, but also are sensitive and show concern with how their actions affect others.

Accountability cannot be handled informally. While starting out with any new venture an accountability plan has to be in place. At the outset, management needs to meet with team members, and firmly charter goals and associated time lines. Channels of communication need to be created and maintained, both for individual and team accountability. A clear plan stating the chain of command and reporting details is essential, as the accountability of any team ultimately affects other teams and departments, and eventually its organization. Another important aspect that any team and its facilitator need to remember is that diffusion of accountability does not demean individual accountability; rather it redefines it by including the team accountability dimension.

'You do what I tell you to do when I tell you to do it'—this has always worked previously, as most of the aspects were handled by a team manager alone and there was no clear-cut demarcation of responsibilities. But now, due to the introduction of the concept of empowerment and the acceptance of the fact that all work is teamwork, the bridge between chaos and stability has proved to be accountability. Teams are empowered to decide for themselves. Teams can choose how they organize themselves. They can make and meet their own goals.

The trade-off for all this empowerment is accountability. The management must not feel bothered about what and how employees do to fulfill the commitments, as long as they *consistently* deliver business value.

9.2 The Collective Accountability Approach—'Only and Only Performance Matters'

The domain of personal responsibility
Must be extended to team responsibility
In order to ensure
Fulfillment of collective accountability.

The Collective Accountability Approach states that if all are committed to a certain goal, then all are also required to be accountable for the output, both success and failure. Individual team members are not only accountable for individual competence but also for the overall team output.

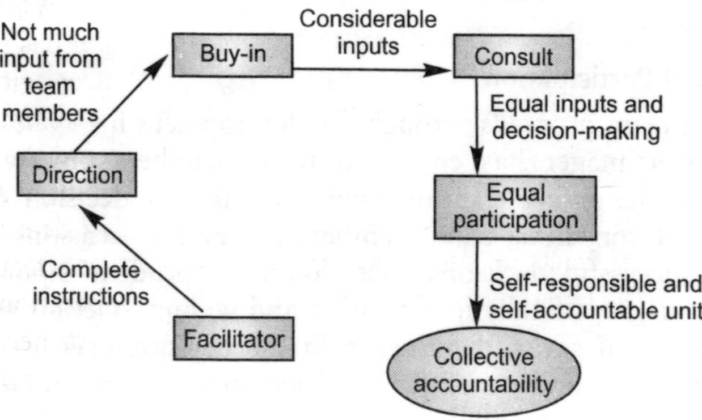

Fig. 9.2: The 5-step Cycle of Accountability

Initially, when the SDWT is formed, it needs to go through a five-step cycle in order to secure itself as a capable unit, to bear the burden of *trust* and *accountability*.

A. Direction

Team managers give instructions to and direct a team in every little aspect. Giving minute details happens in the initial phases of the team building process and they also steer a team in organization-related matters. Direction giving is about 'Making the team comfortable.'

B. Buy-in

Team managers make decisions and then present the rationale behind the decision to the concerned team. They put forward the decision details, and seek a buy-in and commitment from team members. Buy-in usually occurs when a team manager has to take decisions all by himself, which solely fall under his scope, but have influence on his team and its performance. Buy-in can be termed as 'Judicious Inputs' too.

C. Consult

Team managers invite suggestions for arriving at a decision and after seeking inputs from team members, they take the final call. Consulting is one way of ensuring team members get groomed to take their own decisions later on in the development life cycle, something that I call 'Readiness Assurance'.

D. Equal Participation

As a team proceeds through the development life cycle and its team manager has consulted team members on several occasions, he invites team members to make the decision with him. After consulting team members on several occasions and taking successful decisions based on their prudent inputs, a team manager is finally in a position and willing to let his team have an equal say and influence in the decision-making and accountability process. Equal participation is the road to 'Synergistic Accountability'.

E. Self-accountable Unit

After a tried and tested period of equal participation, a team manager hands over the accountability to his team, and this is when his team becomes a self-accountable unit in the true sense. Here, team managers only facilitate the process by having a feedback loop attached to timelines in order to keep track of team accountability and whether it meets the expectations of a team. This is what we can term as 'Integrated Ownership' too.

Empowerment is the process of enabling and authorizing a team to think, take action, execute and control work in an autonomous way. It is the state of feeling self-empowered to take control of a team's own operations. The collective approach achieves exactly this. The six phases of the team life cycle correspond to steps mentioned earlier:

Direction —> Sub-phase 1: In this stage, a team manager needs to direct team members regarding team goals and roles. Although people seem to agree on the superficial level but undercurrents of misinterpretations are predominantly present, and this is where a team manager steps in by making the right decisions. A team manager is fully accountable for his team actions.

Buy-in —> Sub-phase 2: In this stage, a team manager needs to make quick rational decisions to pull team members in one direction, to put an end to all the disagreements. Here a team manager has to be directive and also be fair by seeking commitment and agreement from his team by being open to them.

Consult —> Sub-phase 3: In this stage, a team manager begins to seek inputs and lessens the direction level. Team members begin to understand their team goals and their roles clearly, and they are given additional responsibilities. A team manager consults his team members so that they can carry out their responsibilities and also be accountable for the same.

Equal Participation —> Sub-phase 4: In this stage, a team manager continues to coach his team but only in very critical matters, whereas in all other issues there is equal participation and equal influence in the decision making, thereby expanding a team's boundary of accountability.

Self-accountable unit —> Sub-phases 5 and 6 of the results phase: Team managers step back and let their teams to become fully self-directing and self-accountable. By the time team members reach the results phase, they are fully coached and ready to take on leadership roles, are open to rotation of roles and are capable of making an organization wide impact.

9.3 Exit the Blame Game—'No Room for Ulterior Motives'

Constant coordination
Eliminates the culture
Of seeking scapegoats
And all undercurrents it filters.

To minimize accountability conflicts, contradictory opinions regarding roles, answerability and chain of command must be eliminated. Accountability conflicts don't necessarily mean discomfort but they could lead to ambiguity, if they are poorly managed. Ambiguity related to accountability affects productivity, lowers morale and generates more conflict. It is important for each team member to focus forward on accountability, and not backward on blame or excuse.

The tips listed as follows build accountability within teams:

A. Regular review of role descriptions is crucial. Get your employee's input to the reviews. A team manager needs to make sure that team members understand how their personal accountability plugs into team accountability, and finally how team accountability fits into the big picture of their organization.

B. Clearly set expectations for each team member are necessary, to ensure that they operate within their accountability limits and do not cross into others' operational boundaries, thereby ensuring that accurate reporting of work output occurs. This accuracy also ensures that each team member is rewarded in accordance with his expectations and accountability levels. There is no chance of inaccurate work measurements being reported.

C. For new hires, workshops are needed to get them on the same page of understanding as far as responsibilities and the command chain is concerned. If an organization fails to provide the necessary support, then the new hires can indulge in finger pointing or challenge existing norms as they feel left out of the empowerment process.

D. If teams are truly taking ownership and reflect it through measurable results, then this goes to show that they are willing to raise their own bar by expanding the periphery of accountability, and the management needs to install adequate provisions to encourage this kind of mentality.

E. Regularly hold meetings to communicate new initiatives and status of current development so that employees have a clear picture of their accountability status.

F. Each team member must do his/her part. In team efforts, no team member is unimportant, and has skills supported by other team members. Even if one team member is missing, it is bound to affect the productivity levels adversely. Thus, each team member needs to be given his fair share of accountability.

G. When a team has gone through the 5-step cycle, at least once, and the roles and expectations have been set and the management has provided the required tools, support and training, then top executives are required to 'let the teams do their work'. The management needs to avoid controlling every little work decision of teams through the micromanage mode.

It is quintessential for the aspect of accountability to be free of positional biases so as to leverage the collective wisdom of the entire team.

9.3.1 Example—'The Cat and Mouse Game'

Problem Statement

It has been four months since his promotion to a program lead, and Ron is frustrated with the way things are going for him. Talking to another team lead, "I don't know how to handle the blame game. If the team succeeds then everyone enjoys a share in it, but if it fails then I am the only one to be blamed," said an agitated Ron. "Have you spoken to your team manager about this?," asked his colleague. Ron told him that there are no proper reporting and delegation checkpoints in place. "My team manager and I had just a brief meeting of 15 minutes on delegation but that did not really serve the purpose. I mean what information I can share with my team, when I am not well informed about my role," replied Ron.

Apparently, Ron's team manager trusts well enough to think Ron can handle all this and can manage the team without much direction.

Problem Analysis

Ron's situation is a tough one to be in. His team manager seems to believe that by merely appointing Ron as program lead, his duty as a team manager is over. He fails to understand that due to the lack of clear direction and constant communication, Ron is overwhelmed with the blame game and the team dynamics are not in place. The main reason for Ron's frustration is that his team manager has never been able to realize the importance of clear delegation of assignments. Due to this, other team members do not feel empowered and trusted, and hence put all the blame on the newly appointed lead.

To be able to build a team-driven culture, every team manager needs to ensure that proper ground rules (for the various aspects of team building) must be developed and shared appropriately. Team managers are required to become team builders rather than yet another religious follower of hierarchy.

Solution

The team manager must arrange for formal training and discussion for the program lead and rest of the team members to build a high performance team.

It is imperative for team managers to make sure that the reporting and delegation chain is in place. By encouraging team members to share leadership, puts an end to group politics and the blame game is reduced drastically.

A vital part of a team manager's duty is to delegate tasks, along with a sense of ownership and authority to make decisions related to the delegated tasks. Entrusting team members with both responsibility and authority makes each employee answerable for both types of outcomes—success and failure.

9.3.2 Worksheet for Eliminating the Blame Game

Individual Accountability Level

The Individual Accountability Level worksheet figures out whether or not a particular team member exceeded expectations in the areas of accountability and responsibility, and helps to design corrective mechanisms accordingly.

Team Member Name: Role and Responsibilities: Team Manager's remarks: Accepts accountability for own decisions, actions and results (sample remarks)		
Area	Specific performance results/examples	Additional Notes
Willingness to take risks and solve problems in order to fulfill the responsibilities		
Does the team member ever indulge in the blame game in order to avoid being accountable for the failure		
Even in times of delegation does the		

(Contd...)

team member stick by the process and accepts ownership for the results—success or failure		
Does the team member own up for mistakes and also shows the willingness to learn from the mistakes		
Level of reliability on the team member for completing the designated tasks		
Does the team member create an environment of collective accountability by leading members by example		
Provides support in times of performance breakdowns		

9.4 Eliminating Dysfunctions—'Collective Buy-in is the Key to Collective Ownership'

Team building is the perfect antidote
For dysfunctions,
Leaving no room for office politics.

Any accountability disagreement must be discussed and not deteriorate into personal attacks. The reporting patterns, roles and their descriptions designed in the kickoff meeting, can be used as a reference to clarify any overlaps in accountability. Each team needs to be constantly reminded that accountability is not about individual ownership but about collective answerability. They should be reminded of their common purpose, goals, and the importance of improving team involvement and participative management.

In today's times, organizations expect team members to put in more efforts. If organizations are going to expect more from teams, then they must also be willing to give them more.

The right kind of support, rewards, regular feedback, tools and training is the key to motivate employees to put in their best.

When thinking about empowering teams, it is crucial that the management avoids thinking of it as something that needs to be explicitly handled or bestowed on. Rather, it is essential, to groom team members through the collective accountability approach, by handing them more responsibilities and assigning additional roles through the various phases of development. This makes people realize that their accountability index is increasing and they automatically feel more responsible, and hence more accountable. This goes to show that empowerment is something that comes from within each and every team member. The main role of the management is to find ways to foster the ability of the SDWTs to operate in empowered ways.

9.5 Chapter Recap

1. Accountability is the name of the game. A team feels mutually accountable to each other and accepts collective ownership of the consequences that come with this group accountability.
2. Mutual enrichment creates a culture of peer-to-peer accountability. Clarity, mutual agreement and cooperation effortlessly engage everyone and keep them on track from beginning to end.
3. Direction, Buy-in, Consultation, Equal participation and finally a self-accountable unit is the roadmap that any team needs to follow through all the phases, to grow into a mature, mutually accountable unit.
4. Accountability, in other words, is traceability. This traceability eliminates the blame game, negativity and finger pointing. The only way to make a team member's contribution more visible is by rewarding not only his efforts but also his accountability.
5. The only way that an organization can eliminate accountability dysfunctions is by speaking a common language, "Let's overcome the dysfunctions in unison as we are equally accountable."

10

Motivation-Driven Model of Results—'The Essence of Team Efforts'

Results are derived from disciplined choices,
And disciplined choices
Are derived from motivated efforts.

Joint working efforts produce performance-concentrated results. Results are not just about meeting financial targets or crossing a particular figure, but rather about focusing on performance to tap opportunities which leads to success cycles. The motivation-driven model of results has four main aspects to it: Mission Statement, Healthy Interdependence, Motivation factors and Criteria.

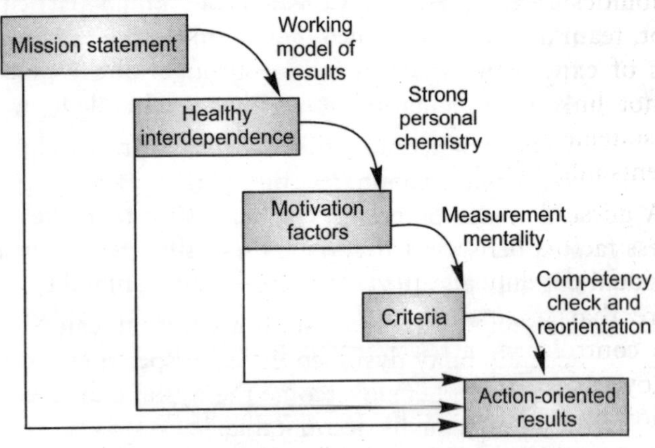

Fig. 10.1: Motivation-Driven Model of Results

An SDWT needs to know what outcome is expected, where its work contributes to the goal, how well things are progressing, and what to do if results are not as they are expected to be. This is where the above model fits in. Once a team aligns itself to the mission statement, team members then become more willing to coordinate their efforts with each other. To maintain this healthy interdependence, every coaching manager needs to make use of several motivation factors. Along with these factors, several criteria need to be used to regulate whether or not a team needs further tuning. Once these four facets are in place, then every factor by itself can generate the desired results. Every SDWT has to go through this cycle at least once to bring about the agreed results.

10.1 Mission Statement—'Stand by Your Purpose'

A Mission statement is the ideals
By which each organization stands for
And each SDWT strives for.

The mission statement is one of the prime factors in designing a working model of excellence for each team. This in turn, motivates team members to align their working towards it and ensure improvement in results.

A strongly worded Mission Statement rules out all possibilities of ego clashes, technical and social hang ups. No doubt, team members are functional experts in their respective areas of expertise, but unless their strengths and weaknesses are not linked to the model, they are not going to deliver. The statement of objectives establishes standardization, which prevents unnecessary re-iteration through the motivation cycle.

A mission statement is the reflection of the challenges and success factors that affect team results. It also acts as inputs to individual development plans that each team member tracks to ensure that his contribution is in place. Mission statement gives control over actual performance of activities. Once the employees understand how their work is going to affect the mission and which part of the mission they are supposed to focus on, team managers then need not exercise excessive control mechanism. Reinforcing the mission statement from time to time, ensures that team members learn to perform efficiently and can be empowered to perform autonomously.

Another important aspect of the mission statement is that it pinpoints the various performance areas and lets a team manager decide on the delegation levels. This instills the drive to perform, across all levels. The interlinked performance factor motivates each team member to put in their best, as they know even if one link fails the entire project is bound to be affected, negatively. As each team member has equal empowerment and has a strong sense of self-esteem, no one is ready to fail.

10.1.1 Example—'The Tunnel-vision Mission'

Problem Statement

The current mission statement of a particular product development team reads "The mission of our organization is to grow rapidly using innovation to beat all competition". This statement does not act as a strong driver. Since it is stated in generic terms, team members fail to understand what their exact goals and future vision are.

Problem Analysis

The above statement merely focuses on the present, and does not pay attention to the future of the organization and its employees. There is no clear roadmap that it provides. Since the statement itself has a limited vision, naturally, the team too maintains the same level of vision.

It does not contain elements of the future, and hence does not support the philosophy of continual progress and learning. Example of a correctly framed statement could read as follows: "Our aim is to double sales this quarter. We plan on accomplishing this goal by devoting time for learning sales and negotiation skills, and then applying the same for striking lucrative deals. Our ultimate mission is to provide consistently attractive returns and become a dominant player in the field of telecommunication."

Solution

A mission statement not only reflects corporate level goals, but also has elements that relate to team member aspirations. They need to be formed meticulously with power words. While building and developing the statement, inputs from team members reinforces team focus.

Mission statement is not just a 20 minutes activity. Adequate time and thinking is necessary to develop a concise and accurate one, which covers all aspects of an organization —people, processes, values and visions.

10.1.2 Worksheet for Creating the Mission Statement

Mission Statement

The Mission Statement worksheet analyzes the effectiveness of the organizational vision. The responses determine whether or not it reflects the core of the project that a particular team has been assigned to. The responses help team members to figure out whether the main questions are addressed or not—Who are we, What are we supposed to accomplish and What do we stand for?

Organization:
Organization vision:
Does the mission statement reflect the anticipated outcomes?
Does the mission statement provide a basis for evaluating the outcomes?

Item	Description
Philosophy of the Management	Specific, measurable and future-driven Vision/ Mission Statement
Processes, Practices	Processes, policies and practices needed to support this philosophy
Positive Peer Culture	Support structures needed to maintain and sustain shared beliefs and values
Teams	How will teams be involved in realizing the organizational mission
The Key Strategic Areas	New market areas, geographic domain, venture capital, stock options for teams
Corporate Values	Values related to innovation, customer returns, recognition, products, technology

(Contd...)

Action Programs	Research and development, seek industrial expertise
Tools and Technology	Tools and mechanisms for measuring success
Goals to be achieved	Does the mission statement reflect clear-cut and measurable goals
Ethical stand	What is the exact public image that the organization wants to portray
Can the team members articulate the mission statement clearly	Do team members relate to the mission and find it meaningful and important

10.2 Healthy Interdependence—'Integrate Uniqueness'

Strong personal chemistry
Aligns resources
And maintains team unity, for ages.

In current times, most of the organizations operate at the global level. To succeed in this era of global competition, these organizations need to have several major subsystems in place, and that too well integrated. To achieve this macro level integration, interdependence at the micro level is a must. Interdependence at the team level leads to the development of highly coupled subsystems. Healthy interdependence is about coupling at all levels—upstream, lateral and downstream.

Positive interdependence is an important aspect of a successful team environment that brings out the best in each team member. Healthy interdependence taps into the collective knowledge of an SDWT. Team members feed off of each other's knowledge to develop ideas, which both in numbers and quality, far exceed than those of any individual team member or their traditional counterparts. Interdependence also raises and addresses problems at the right time. As people have developed mutual trust and empathy, they are confident that even if they admit their weaknesses and mistakes they are not going to be reprimanded, but instead be mentored and motivated. Thus, healthy interdependence encourages people to be authentic, which in turn helps teams to stay on track.

Conflict and competition are key factors for growth but then they have their own downside. Many times, if the competition is too tight or the conflict is extreme, they are either ignored or used as means of criticizing each other. Hence, if they are replaced with healthy interdependence then there is nothing like it.

Unbiased peer feedback is a crucial element in building mutually beneficial relationships. Feedback needs to change from 'you need to work hard' to 'you are competent and can achieve more'. With such healthy feedback, teams can accomplish *incremental* improvement in their results and the results of their organization as well. By respecting each other as unique individuals and accepting each others' strengths and weaknesses without holding any subjective opinions, helps team members to learn how to recognize and benefit from their differences. Each interface that nurtures interdependence needs personalized attention and optimization.

One of the most indelible advantages of an integrated team is that sub-problem solutions are derived to form a well-designed output, which means no one operates in isolation. The management has to consider various factors like organizational culture, leadership styles, processes and personality differences, before designing tools for forging strong interdependent links. Integrative influence is a direct by-product of healthy interdependence, thereby promoting organizational democracy.

10.2.1 Example—'Another Bump on the Road to the Finish'

Problem Statement

In the 360 degrees feedback, Jane reported on her colleague Jess, stating that she is an underperformer, who disrupts the team functioning and should not be considered for any kind of promotion at all. All the other employees have stated otherwise, they have rated Jess as a star performer and Jane as a non-performer. From these responses, one can easily sense unhealthy interdependence and an atmosphere of cross-agendas.

Problem Analysis

The team manager never confronted this difficult behavior and performance issues head on. The team also did not bring to his notice the unhealthy interdependence between Jess and Jane, which in turn was affecting the entire team. They knew all along that Jane was the trouble maker, whereas Jess was their star performer. Due to this extreme difference and Jane's contemptuous attitude, team members had decided not to bring it out in the open. But their responses in the feedback had made things clear.

Jane, out of sheer insecurity is not able to appreciate her colleague's plus points, and fears that the team is eventually going to let the management know that she is not a team player. Therefore, she uses the feedback as an opportunity to belittle Jess.

Solution

First, the team manager and his team needs to have a discussion (without Jess and Jane) to identify the nature of conflict, the reasons, and draw out an intervention plan to deal with this unhealthy interdependence. Then, the team manager needs to have a one-one session with Jane and Jess to bring about a consensus in working. The team manager must keep in touch with them on a regular basis, and must hone group process facilitation skills to avoid rude surprises. A systematic step-by-step process needs to be implemented on a consistent basis, to allow team members to work in a healthy dependence mode.

10.2.2 Worksheet for Developing Healthy Interdependence

Healthy Interdependence

The Healthy Interdependence worksheet assists the SDWT to identify and work on areas like cooperation skills, mutually responsible behavior and other aspects needed in maintaining a healthy environment.

<table>
<tr><td colspan="3">Team Member Name:
Team Manager's notes:</td></tr>
<tr><td>Item</td><td>Response</td><td>Action tools</td></tr>
<tr><td>Rate the team interdependence</td><td>Sample response: Healthy, Unhealthy</td><td></td></tr>
<tr><td>Positive aspects of the interdependence</td><td></td><td></td></tr>
<tr><td>Needs which are not being met</td><td></td><td></td></tr>
<tr><td>Rationale behind team members taking different stands</td><td></td><td></td></tr>
<tr><td colspan="3">Which qualities you value in the relationship with:
Team Member # 1
Team Member # 2
Team Member # 3</td></tr>
<tr><td colspan="3">Ratings for various interdependence factors:
1 = Perfect, 2 = Change Required, 3 = Present, 4 = Absent
• Is Team Morale present
• Is Politics and Power play present
• Do attitudes and behavioral patterns need a change
• Do team norms need an overhaul
• Is retraining required
• Is constructive discussion happening
• Is change in rewards and recognition required
• Do team members care for each other
• Any other observations</td></tr>
</table>

10.3 Motivation—'Move into Action'

Motivation leads
to action-oriented partnerships.
Motivation leads
to an upward spiral of super wins.

A. Measurement Mentality

There has to be some way for a team to see what others are doing on a weekly basis. This can be in the form of results log, activity reports, work schedules or other reports.

Keeping a log of results, people accountable for them and what exactly transpired reinforces the performance levels. This log instills a self-check loop and provides increased visibility of work, something that I refer to as 'Measurement Mentality.'

Using the above log or any form of results recording system, a team can rate its team members based on their strengths, and reward the results that they have delivered. Team managers need to reconfigure themselves into performance coaches, who fuel work motivation and personal pride through their positive feedback.

B. Team Profile

A team profile is an effective practice of maintaining team motivation. Relevant behavioral disciplines and patterns for every team member need to be set up. For doing so, the questionnaire method can be used. The responses collected through the questionnaire can be used to find out the compatibility levels and attitudes. Using these inputs, a team manager is able to decide on how to motivate team members, and how to encourage them to build synergy and complementary skills. In short, profile analysis of the SDWT enables to find the gap and work on designing motivation methods, to bring the incompatible behaviors closer to the profile baseline. By closing this gap, team members are able to perform better, and their performance itself acts as a fuel to their motivation levels.

C. Morale Boosters

In the regular status update meeting, a slot for airing appreciative comments for results can be reserved. Apart from the official dose of motivation, an organization can also plan for outdoor activities to reinforce the appreciation by either arranging a pizza outing or a comp-off. Moral uplifts can also mean letting team members have their way of executing their responsibilities, as long as they give the best results. Even discussing the rich working history and the strong profile of team members every now and then works wonders.

D. Mutual Support and Trust

Team members have to constantly feed their trust and support by reminding each other of their past history of successful results, how they have backed each other through thick and thin, and how they have stood the test of challenges in unison.

With mutual trust, team members learn to know other team members' strengths and weaknesses and learn to work the issue, not the person.

E. Task Interdependence

Reasonable and well laid down task-level interactions prove that affective outcomes are stronger, as team members are linked to each other due to task integration structures. This integration motivates team members to perform well as each individual contribution not only affects the individual outputs of others but also the collective result. As task-related performance goals change over the life cycle of a team, the best practices need to be adjusted accordingly, only then the results will be reproducible.

In order to repeat successful exercises, team members must be able to see that the same actions needed to complete the tasks be repeated, which in turn leads to the same results. Developing fundamental capabilities is the process which yields the same result every time, and analysis of the same finds out where the difference lies. This difference can be nullified by rethinking of areas where improvements can still be made.

F. Warm up Activities

One of the most important activities at the very start of the team formation process, even before teams start working is an ice breaker session, where team members are introduced to each other and are allowed to share their information. Team members indulge in asking each other open-ended questions. As time progresses, they begin to share a certain comfort level and can take up other activities to build a brand for themselves in terms of team names, logos or taglines. These team-related symbols keep them motivated and develop an *esprit de corps*.

Management needs to give SDWTs lots of time and space, since generating results is not a process that can be forced upon.

10.3.1 Example—'Bright but Not Right'

Problem Statement

Cindy was a bright but dissatisfied business analyst in the capital markets domain. "Cindy, tomorrow and the day after, you will need to collect and collate responses to the employee satisfaction survey from the team," said Gus curtly, Cindy's team manager. "Sir, I have already done that so many times in the past, I really want to do something very challenging, something that will enhance my learning graph," pleaded Cindy. Cindy was not particularly thrilled with this non-contributing assignment and she wanted to discuss her reservations. Gus dismissed the meeting without giving Cindy a chance to discuss her views. Cindy left the cabin fuming with dissatisfaction.

Gus felt satisfied that as a team manager he was doing all he could do to motivate his team, by assigning extra roles and assignments.

Problem Analysis

Cindy is not happy with her new assignment as it does not meet her growth goals, and hence is not motivated enough to take it on with commitment. In her last one-one session with her team manager, she had clearly mentioned that she wants to take up higher assignments, and not just reviews or surveys. Her team manager was not able to comprehend her aspirations and individual goals, and his lack of understanding leads to this assignment mismatch.

Gus's baseless assumption of merely assigning new roles/tasks without any discussion of employee aspirations, leads to team dissatisfaction rather than motivation.

Solution

Each team manager needs to have a one-one session with each team member on a regular basis. He must set aside 15-25 minutes for each individual every month, to get a feel of new aspirations, goals and expectations. From these sessions, a team manager can gather essential details about individual aspirations regarding their career and personal growth. These inputs aid team managers to assign the right roles to the right people. Intelligent assignment leads to the satisfaction of personal needs of team members. When team members realize that the roles assigned to them fulfill their hopes and needs, they put in their best and deliver positive results. They take pride in their role, and this in turn leads to group motivation and high team morale.

10.3.2 Worksheet for Motivation

Maintaining Motivation

The Maintaining Motivation worksheet helps to identify categories and subcategories where the employees are not motivated enough to give their peak performance.

Motivation Factors	Rating and Progress Level	Corrective Measures
Progress Level — 'A'=Achieved, 'I'=In Progress, 'Y'=Yet to implement		
Freedom:		
Job enrichment and job enlargement opportunities		
Opportunities and space for the employees to work as per their own decisions and sense of judgment		
Encouragement is given based on individual preferences and work-related values		
Opportunities for growth at the macro level, being a part of the big picture		
Freedom to adopt innovative methods of performing tasks whereby the chances of		

(Contd...)

survival increase		
Opportunities provided for synergistic combinations of ideas and abilities		
Recognition:		
Regular dose of verbal appreciation		
Tangible rewards in the form of promotions, incentives, compensatory offs, bonus		
Recognition for team managers too, who have aided in building a high performance team		
Balance:		
Balance between work and home		
Addressing the needs of team members, both personal and professional		
Joint activities outside the organization to include employee families		
Honest Practices:		
Equal and fair treatment to everyone		
Challenging targets for all		
Open atmosphere for receiving and giving feedback		
Assurance that every employee's suggestions for improving the working environment will be given due consideration		
Examples:		
Remind employees of their past success		
Narrate success stories of other teams		
Share motivational quotes,		

(Contd…)

posters, include team achievements in in-house journals		

10.4 Criteria—'Keep Track of Motivation Levels'

Consolidating results on a periodic basis is the key to keeping team members' competence levels at an all-time high.

10.4.1 Competence Check and Potential Analysis

Regular checks keep the team atmosphere motivated. Clearly stated answers to the questions as follows, provide feedback and deviation details:

Does the team feel that it has the right people on board?
Does the team feel that its team members have the apt skills and competence?

Answers to these questions either reinforce the positive results or enable a team to find the right kind of strategies, resources and tools to reorient itself, in order to feel motivated to accomplish the mission statement.

Team members are not only expected to monitor results but also take the actions required to produce those results. The success parameters along with deviations must be constantly checked.

Team members need to maintain their own personal marketing plans. Each team member's plan sets out the details of the contribution that he is required to make to his team's overall success. As each team member has a clear roadmap, they know what they are supposed to focus on, thereby ensuring that nobody goes about nose poking, but rather concentrates on the work assigned to them.

10.4.2 Checklists

A vital criterion for reinforcing motivation is to design checklists for tasks and key processes. They have to be updated to be in sync with any changes as this ensures continuous improvement. The checklists need to be conformed to every single time for every single task. The changes to the checklists need to be done in consultation with a team manager and his team members.

10.5 Advantages of Motivation-Driven Model of Results

A. Healthy interdependence makes communication transparent, and the right information available at the right place, right time and in the right quantity.

B. The model transforms random group efforts into collaborative teamwork.

C. Mission Statement integrates individual vision statements into one team-vision statement.

D. Healthy interdependence generates a whole spectrum of positive team experiences, which further strengthens the bonds.

E. Motivation factors create and maintain the atmosphere of 'Coordinated Responsibility' for the entire project period, right from concept to market.

10.6 Chapter Recap

1. A strong mission statement creates a motivational context within which a team operates in a focused manner.
2. In order to develop a well-aligned team, healthy interdependence needs to be fostered through common agendas, frustrations, problems and aspirations.
3. Motivation is not about technology. It's not about great gifts. It's about creating committed linkages between team members. Motivation is the key to both task accomplishment and team building.
4. Performing regular checks on the motivation levels, lets organizations fine-tune their motivation policy. Consolidating results on a periodic basis is the key to keeping team members' competence levels at an all-time high.

11

The FACT Model for Team Effectiveness—'Catalyze the Concept of Working as a Whole'

Being self-conscious
About its own purpose
Is what makes a self-directed work team
An outstanding team.

The FACT model is more than a simple four step process for *correcting* team gaps. It is an effective means for creating a springboard for enhanced performance. This model is all about *creating* and *sustaining* results. Enhancing team effectiveness is not about paying enough but about rewarding appropriately.

Fig. 11.1: The FACT Model for Team Effectiveness

This model is about striking a balance between immediate goals with long-term targets towards the vision of an organization. Facilitators, a proper mix of tools and cognitive analysis lead to the next generation of self-motivated, self-initiated facilitators. The team performance rises to another level altogether.

11.1 Facilitators—'Great Coaches Train Themselves First, Then the Team'

Facilitation = Creating + Building + Sustaining Teams

Facilitation is about support and mediation, and not about decision-making. Facilitators are expected to possess strong group process skills, and act as mentors who share their knowledge and make a team aware of the office protocols.

Facilitators need to work at two levels, first as a 'team member,' where they guide team efforts to achieve short-term goals and second as a 'strategic specialist,' where they steer team initiatives to bring about organizational growth.

One of the most important facilitators is the team manager. A team manager must be able to coach, problem-solve, gain consensus and mediate during conflicts whenever necessary. Team managers/leaders help team members to level their interests. Also, they balance differing views so that team goals succeed over personal interests.

Along with the top management inputs, a team manager needs to review and approve several processes. Executive guidance is needed to redirect a team toward its goals and motivate it to maintain group focus. Facilitation offers the opportunity to model effective leadership and related skills to team members. Facilitation implies only corrective direction and not coercive force.

11.1.1 Example—'The Careless Coach'

Problem Statement

After three months of joining, a review from team members on the new team coach Dan was conducted, which revealed a below average rating for the facilitation skills of the new coach. The team manager and his team were called in by the top executives, to discuss this gap between the expectations of team members from the team manager and the team manager's performance.

At the end of the meeting, the reasons for why the new coach and team members were not on the same page of understanding had become crystal clear. According to the team, their team manager did not encourage them, never empowered them and did not communicate with them. The new team manager had come from an organization where the leadership style was more hierarchy-driven, and hence he was not aware of the leadership dynamics in the new setting. He assumed that everyone will do just as they are told to do by him and there was no need of constant communication.

Problem Analysis

Due to the lack of proper facilitation of the team manager himself, there was unrest in the team, and this was aggravated by his lack of understanding of facilitative leadership skills. The top management did not give much time for the team manager to settle down in his new post, and hence the team was not able to accommodate him. At the same time, his past way of functioning also got in the way of smooth functioning in his new job. The lack of a supportive top management is also instrumental for this fallout.

Due to the heavy handed leadership style adopted by the new team manager, conflicts were bound to occur. The new manager treated his team members as subordinates and did not give them empowerment opportunities, which in turn affected the otherwise knowledgeable resources and their performance.

Solution

At the outset, the top management needs to give out clear instructions to team managers as to how to achieve a self-directed team culture. Detailed team building implementation plans need to be designed and tracked closely.

The new team manager needs to get rid of any inappropriate anchorages that he has carried over from his previous organization; he must start afresh in the new organization, and be willing to learn its ways without any irrational opinions or biases.

Every team manager and his team must sit down together, and work out detailed improvement plans and clearly share their expectations of each other. In order to adopt a facilitative style of leadership, a team manager needs to understand and appreciate the new policies, procedures, employee interface strategies. He needs to don several hats depending on the situation he has to tackle. Spending quality time with team members to get a feel of their strengths, weaknesses and personalities is useful to a manager.

11.1.2 Worksheet for Facilitators

Degree of Facilitation

The Degree of Facilitation is a worksheet that is filled in by team members. The responses to the various factors ascertain the level of mentoring and training a team manager requires for becoming a perfect team coach. The responses collected can be anonymous or non-anonymous. It helps the executive sponsor to develop a clear picture of the strengths and weaknesses of the concerned team manager's leadership style, and to design a leadership development plan to improve him in the areas where he is lagging behind.

Team Manager Name: Leadership style: Strengths and weaknesses:				
Facilitation factors	Rating	Supporting evidence	What would you like the coach to introduce to enhance the effectiveness of the team	Skills missing
Process-related qualities:				
Manages Conflicts				
Supports new ideas				
Demonstrates effective processes—time				

(Contd...)

management, feedback, decision-making				
A strong knowledge base				
Recognizes outstanding performance				
Soft skills and personality traits:				
Encourages team members, brings out the best in them				
Good communicator, great negotiator				
Discipline is his forte, a perfect role model				
Whether a team builder				
Demonstrates consistency				
Has personal integrity and deals with honesty				
Strives for excellence always				
Additional factors:				
Service before self				
Sets and enforces norms				
Commitment work plans and the success of the team				

11.1.3 Advantages of Facilitators

A. Define the team's standards
B. Champion and sponsor the team's vision
C. Equalize participation
D. Review ground rules
E. Organize team meetings and communication channels
F. Lead the team through performance challenges
G. Manage issues
H. Devolve authority to the teams
I. Coach team members
J. Overcome team barriers

For the above advantages to accrue, the facilitators must develop a range of transferable skills for the workplace, increase their own awareness of team dynamics and hone their skills of facilitation.

11.2 A Combination Approach of Tools—'The Foundation of Cooperation'

In knowledge-based organizations
SDWTs are the norm,
Which keep organizations
Always in a competitive form.

Facilitators along with a combination approach, leverage the advantages of several tools, which are an effective facet of collaborative performance.

11.2.1 Reinforcement—'Adopt an Employee-centered Approach'

Reinforcement equates to motivation. Reinforcement conditions behavior and is beneficial to organizations as it fosters a high performance culture in teams.

SDWTs are concerned with building a strong performance base by surmounting obstacles, and team reinforcement in the form of team reward does exactly that. Team reward aims to reinforce behavior that leads to effective teamwork. It encourages group endeavors rather than just individual contributions.

11.2.2 *Tools—'More Dimensions, Wider Views'*

Quality tools such as process analysis or decision-making can help a team to better understand its processes and organize data into workable solutions. Some of the tools that any SDWT can utilize are as follows:

A. **Cause analysis**—helps to identify the root causes of a problem. It aims at eliminating the root causes rather than just the symptoms.

B. **Process analysis**—helps to identify and eliminate unnecessary processes, thereby reducing timelines and cutting down costs. It aids teams in improving the performance of their activities.

C. **Affinity diagram**—a visual tool that organizes a large number of ideas/data using logical relationships. This tool comes in handy during brainstorming sessions.

D. **Decision-making**—helps to make judicious decisions based on an objective rating scale.

E. **Tree diagram**—helps to break down broad categories into levels of detail, helping a team induce the number of possible outcomes and focus on the most desirable outcome.

F. **Matrix diagram**—shows the relationship between two or more than two elements, and analyzes the strengths of their relationships on the basis of certain criteria.

11.2.3 *Prioritizing—'Make Rational Choices'*

Prioritizing is essential to sieve out unnecessary issues, to identify what's important and urgent to a team. Simply put prioritizing is about voting for critical issues. Each team member must be given equal representation in the votes collected. There are several ways of collecting votes:

1. Open voting where team members cast their vote in front of everyone.
2. You can create a list of issues and go around asking for the first choice and place a tick against it. Conduct the same process for subsequent choices.

Based on the results, the most critical issue can be pinpointed.

3. In case of sensitive items, team members can jot down their responses, something like a secret ballot.

With good prioritizing skills, a team is able to allot more time and focus its attention on urgent tasks. Here the main factor which defines the criticality of the task is its returns in the long run. Prioritizing is very useful when a team seems to be pulling in different directions. It is particularly performed where a stable consensus needs to be arrived at. It is a favorable technique for giving each team member fair input, thereby ensuring that his team is not a one man show, but performance put in by collaborative colleagues.

11.2.4 Go-Around—'Keep the Feedback Coming'

In this technique, a team manager sequentially seeks ideas/feedback from each team member. If a particular team member doesn't have anything to contribute, he or she can pass during a round. Team members can also get back in and contribute on subsequent rounds.

It is possible that shy team members can have great ideas but due to their fear of non-conformance they may not open up. Go-around is an effective way of getting introvert team members to contribute. It works wonders with new team members too.

11.2.5 Rating Systems—'Be Objective'

The performance of a team can be measured based on four levels: Novice, Competent, Proficient and Expert. Rating systems isolate performance gaps, motivate team members, and plan strategies for improvement and counseling.

Table 11.1: Level and Action Plan

Level	Action Plan
Novice	Guidance and intensive training
Competent	Guidance and counsel at regular intervals
Proficient	Coach and train as and when required
Expert	Delegate

11.2.6 *Knowledge Management (KM)—'Knowledge Creation, Analysis and Sharing'*

SDWTs are required to constantly tap into their individual experience and knowledge, and then use the collective reserves within the team to design lucrative strategies. Collective insights promise efficient deliverance of results. Knowledge in and knowledge of the process is fragmented. No single person has/group of people have full understanding of the entire process. This is indicative of the potential value of a KM effort, which enables efficient access and sharing of high-quality, relevant, timely knowledge—up, down, and across organizational lines, especially those functional and organizational lines that result in fragmented processes.

The points listed as follows are necessary for implementing KM for improving teams:

1. Develop basic process competence.
2. List down missing metrics.
3. Consider benchmarking.
4. Work to diffuse internal knowledge/practices.
5. Provide supportive learning environment.
6. Address known knowledge gaps.
7. Check/recheck assumptions.
8. Make the implicit explicit.
9. Learn from malfunctions.

Group collaboration tools like computer-mediated conferences and databases can be used to capture, store, disseminate and apply the knowledge reserves. The elements that form the substance of a quality-oriented KM are —> Define knowledge requirements, Obtain existing knowledge assets, Identify knowledge gaps, Address knowledge gaps to fulfill requirements, and continually preserve and expand knowledge to reflect dynamic requirements. Thus, KM is a continuum perspective, since it constantly converts data into wisdom.

This knowledge management complements and enhances other organizational initiatives such as total quality management, business process re-engineering and organizational learning. It then begins to provide a new and urgent focus to sustain the competitive position and enhance the quality aspect too.

Knowledge Management can be described as the application of knowledge management practices to achieve quality management principles that include customer focus, leadership, involvement of people, process approach, systems approach to management, continual improvement, factual approach to decision-making, and mutually beneficial relationships. All of these finally map to team performance.

Any team's performance is therefore heavily dependent on how team members put this collaboration into action, as it is the most valuable intangible asset for surviving in the global environment.

11.2.7 Example—'Loss of Intellectual Capital is the Biggest Loss'

Problem Statement

Kim, a new entrant with a high profile resume was the source of insecurity for her much senior counterparts on the team. They had no means to compete with her, except for using underhand tactics like not sharing knowledge updates, twisting quality aspects, not including her suggestions in the prioritizing process and making fun of her novel approaches.

After a few months of working, Kim began to lose interest and began underperforming which started affecting the module she was working on, her module was the most important and specialized one. This resulted in a cascade effect; the entire team had to pay a price as their modules were all reliant on Kim's module and its output.

Problem Analysis

The above case clearly indicates that the team coach has not properly planned for the resources. The rest of the team has not taken efforts to build a culture of team success, and hence the team is audacious enough to belittle a high performer.

By indulging in unfair practices, the team is exemplifying the 'We' vs. 'You' attitude. By overlooking all the processes of knowledge management, reinforcement and the various collaboration tools, they are not only hurting an honest and efficient team player, but also jeopardizing their own work and team performance on the whole.

Solution

Firstly, the team coach needs to act as a vigilant resource manager. He needs to realize that team output depends on the cohesive efforts of all the resources. He needs to instill cooperation in the team members so that they constantly monitor and correct their own discrepancies. The most critical duty that he performs as a coach is setting an example by appreciating and applying the tools and processes in a fair manner.

Secondly, team members need to be trained to accommodate new members. Adamant team members need reinforcement in order to play fair and be objective with newcomers. It is very necessary to understand that sharing accurate and timely updates, and also soliciting new inputs is a must for team performance.

For an SDWT to gel well, a connected team manager as well as supportive senior team members are required. Groupism, personal power or authority never ever sort out problems, rather they only compound the problems.

11.3 Cognitive Analysis—'Making Team Knowledge Explicit'

SDWTs are a data-driven knowledge center
Which bring about benefits in tasks, greater.

In order to understand how people perform, it is necessary to understand what goes on inside their heads. Cognitive skills are needed to perform a task at high levels of proficiency. Cognitive task analysis looks at the system from the viewpoint of the user performing a designated task. Cognition is about psychological processes linked to expertise and performance. The rating systems that I talked about earlier are also closely linked to cognitive analysis. It relates to the underlying mental processes, when one undergoes a transformation from novice to expert. The various motivational factors that may contribute to individual differences in outcomes can also be captured through cognitive analysis.

Cognitive analysis begins with an overview of organizational needs followed by mapping out the tasks, logging critical decision points, prioritizing these decisions points, identifying the skills required, data collection, data analysis and decision-making.

There are several cognitive task analysis techniques, and their common aim is to apply expert knowledge to tasks to bring about expert performance. The three main steps involved in any cognitive task analysis tool are:

Knowledge gathering is the process of extracting information, through in-depth interviews and observations, about cognitive events, structures, or models.

Knowledge analysis is the process of structuring data, describing knowledge structures, simplifying, transforming data, and identifying functions involved in the tasks.

Knowledge representation is the process of displaying data, describing relationships and deriving meaning from analysis.

The above three steps transform the output of one's knowledge into process-related views. Generally, one's thinking is translated into viewable observation or verbal cues, but nothing much is known about the internal thinking process, the following mentioned cognitive task analysis techniques help to understand team member's thought processes while performing tasks.

1. **Contextual focus**—Understanding who the team members are, what the objectives are, and what they are going to do to achieve them can form the starting point of any cognitive task analysis exercise. Then one can use other methods to perform further in-depth analysis.

2. **Goal decomposition**—This method focuses on the study and representation of the layers of knowledge that unfold at each level, where each level is mapped to a sub-goal. The level of detail increases as the sub-goals are achieved, thereby providing a close inspection of processes and knowledge required to perform tasks.
3. **Concept maps**—Represent the main idea/theme and the sub-themes in the form of nodes, and the relationships are depicted using links. There are several ways of organizing maps based on a central theme or in order of importance or the flow can be shown with inputs and outputs to interpret a complex concept in a better manner.
4. **Think aloud method**—A method which involves users vocalizing their actions as they perform a set of specified tasks. It is a first-hand experience, and provides insights for the observer to learn about the doer's thoughts and feelings. It is the most direct technique for eliciting and analyzing data which represents a person's knowledge of a task.
5. **Simulation**—A computer-based system that can explain the processes and tasks involved in many team building activities like decision-making and performance assessment.

The above knowledge capture methods enable the process of developing secure decision-making portals. Their analytical and predictive power identifies mental demands needed to perform optimally.

11.3.1 Worksheet for Cognitive Analysis

Task Analysis

The Task Analysis worksheet assists the SDWT to finalize on the tools and knowledge required for performing a particular task and its activities. The responses for all the points in this worksheet assist a team to understand the work patterns and thought processes in a better manner.

Task description: Related processes: Goals of the Task: Performed by Team member, Automated system or a combination: Team Member/s Responsible for the task: If performed by a combination, what are the interfaces between team members and the system: Concept map: What makes this activity easy or difficult:
Sub-Task # 1
Data/Knowledge: Rules and Models: Tools and equipment: Training requirements: Reference documents, standards, checklists: Major inputs and outputs: Rules of thumb: Criticality: Decision rules: Level of difficulty: Performance requirements: Functional elements: Safety Considerations and any other conditions: Attitudes/Skills/Proficiency/Motivation levels:

11.3.2 Advantages of Cognitive Analysis

A. Aids in assessing changes in knowledge base.

B. Better task and interface design is possible, as the analysis information focuses on important tasks and filters out irrelevant information.

C. Useful inputs to the personnel selection process. It aids in identifying key sources of expertise, and gauging a candidate's initiative and responsiveness.

D. Improved planning capability, which lets team members to develop shared task awareness. This ensures that team members plan their work taking into consideration the task sequence, timing, and procedures of every single team member on board.

E. Cognitive task analysis boosts performance by guiding the development of tools that support the cognitive processes.

F. Facilitates progression from one knowledge state to another. Cognitive analysis tools capture missing information bits, pinpoint task-action mismatches, pre-empt potential problems before they arise, and give cues for bottlenecks.

G. Aids in designing comprehensive training and instructions.

11.4 Team-Driven Leaders—'They Exemplify the Vision'

Everyone wants to be a part
Of a dream team.
Only when the right values team leaders impart,
Will such a team come into being.

Purposive learning is the key. Team members imbibe and practise good practices and attitudes from the facilitators, which in turn metamorphose team members into coaching leaders themselves.

The previously discussed three factors generate value-driven team players, along with these factors, the following aspects produce the next generation leaders. SDWTs are not driven by leaders but rather by common values. Team-driven workplace solutions generate the next generation sustainability. Team members want to succeed both as an individual and as a team too. Both team members and facilitators need to concentrate on developing attributes for building a dream team, which are as follows:

A. Performance Standards and Rewards

Each team manager needs to set high standards, but at the same time ensure that each performance is given its due share of praise. Such a team trend tends to keep performance levels high. Staff turnover is low because talented team members recognize that their performance is going to be rewarded, and hence they continue being committed and give their best.

B. Strategic Alignment

Keeping a team focused on corporate goals and missions is not about having a sticky note put up on the wall but rather a way of life. Team members and aspiring future team managers need to experience and imbibe it through the actions and behavior of the facilitators. Lead by example is the *mantra* for producing the next generation team managers. In short, the facilitators through their own actions and decisions must portray that the goal is more important than the role, which helps to create mini corporate groups in the form of cohesive teams.

C. Synergistic Existence Through Shared Values

Develop and support people who care exactly about the same things that an organization cares about. The facilitators have to ensure that the team behavior is in sync with the value statement, corporate culture and formal processes. Team members are required to be trained, to operate in such a way that there is absolutely no room for assumptions, irrational beliefs and taken for granted attitudes.

D. Development

Encouragement from the management in the form of training and skills-upgrade programs, ensures that team members are encouraged to continually develop their personalities and skills. Teams are more than willing to step out of the comfort zone to perform their assigned roles, if they are sure that their personal development needs are taken care of and they have the backing of a strong organizational impetus.

E. Energy and Energize

The culture of energy sharing needs to be in place and constantly fed with mutual trust.

F. Change Agent

The facilitator is the linchpin for change. Management is that change agent, which enables team members to work in a productive manner to achieve the desired results not just in terms of products/services, but which make a productive difference at the organizational level too. Change management allows a team to manage execution of change, which finally gets translated into self-initiated working units.

The new team champions must constantly develop and update a variety of skills and knowledge to ensure successful implementation of team member involvement efforts.

11.4.1 Example—'Surrounded by Suspicion'

Problem Statement

Sally, a very diligent but despondent accountant in the finance department was troubled by the way her immediate team manager was treating her. "This is not right Megan, I put in my best but Robert does not seem to appreciate it." "What's the matter Sally"? asked Megan in an empathetic tone. Sally goes on to tell Megan that each time she completes a task and reports it through the daily update system, her team manager checks on her work through someone else. "He confirms through a third link whether I do my work myself or delegate it to someone else and then report it under my name. It's not fair, I have put four hardworking years in here and this is what I get—distrust. He does not report my performance correctly, and hence I do not get my due share of praise. He seems to feel threatened by my presence in his team."

Megan advised Sally to have a one-one session with her team manager to sort things out, but Sally flatly declined to do so as she does not trust her team manager. "I will not talk to a man who does not lead by example. He doubts the skills of his own team members, and reports information to suit his own personal needs, and uses behind-the-back gossip. I simply don't trust his motives," said Sally angrily.

Problem Analysis

The probable reason for Sally's boss to treat Sally in an unfair manner is his sense of insecurity. He knows that she is a high performer and is capable of taking over his position in the future. The team manager uses stealthy ways to belittle Sally's efforts in order to save his position.

The barriers in communication that he has maintained right from day one is another aspect that has made Sally angry. The most important factor for Sally not trusting her team manager is that he is checking on her work results, which goes to show that he himself is not trustworthy.

Solution

As far as the team manager's sense of insecurity is concerned, he needs to learn to cope with competition and that too in a fair manner. He must reward deserving performance and not undermine it just because he fears demotion or loss of position. To bring to light such faulty managerial patterns, the concerned harassed employee needs to escalate the issue. By keeping quiet, Sally is only adding to her own agony quotient.

Team managers need to realize that team members perform whole-heartedly, only when they have a team manager who trusts them and leads by example. It is important that each team manager works hard at preparing an honest communication system, and neither indulges in gossiping nor encourages others to adopt underhand tactics. Without clear communication and a healthy managerial attitude, solid trust between the two cannot be achieved.

11.5 Chapter Recap

1. Team members are committed to the team vision, whereas team facilitators are more concerned with the team itself, to ensuring the realization of the vision and not the vision itself.
2. A combination approach of practical tools creates team spirit and gets team members into the habit of contributing together. The main aim is to encourage team members to learn to compensate for each other's weaknesses and different personality types, and balance and complement each other. This is exactly what my theory of Perfect Configuration is all about.
3. Cognitive task analysis goes one step beyond traditional job analysis. It focuses on the knowledge and thought processes required to perform the job well. More than the physical workload, what matters is the internal knowledge of the tasks, this attributes a clear-cut meaning to how people think and act.
4. Team-driven leaders are mainly responsible for building a strong commitment level to a common purpose and to achieving a common goal. They are committed to reaping the next level of leaders from within the team itself.

PART IV

Joint Responsibility: It Continues in the Wired World Too

12

Future Trends—'Teams that Win Continuously'

New technology is changing team culture;
It is propelling organizations to the hilt
Of a bright future.

Though the trends (discussed in subsequent paragraphs) have made their presence felt in the business world during the last 10-15 years in a small way, but in the times to come they will be more widely implemented and universally accepted. The future is going to be driven by virtual organizations and self-directed workforces. Organizations have come to realize that the 'silo' mode, and its drawbacks of no shared learning and no mutual support do not work in today's times.

The knowledge-driven economy in today's flat world has opened the gateway to a global talent pool and knowledge sharing. This is significantly going to increase as more and more organizations join the *seamless bandwagon.* But of course, on the one hand, they are excited to have such teams on board, and on the other hand, they are constantly bothered about how to get there. Nevertheless, virtual teams are growing and are becoming an integral part of the business landscape.

Apart from the day-to-day activities and a reasonably high degree of empowerment, teams are slowly and steadily becoming the hubs for organization-level decisions. They are in fact no longer viewed as merely project groups, task force teams or action committees. They have begun to shoulder strategic responsibilities as well. This indicates that there will be a better balance in decision-making. This team autonomy needs to be driven by the management vision, and also heavily depends on the willingness to experiment with this kind of a performance model.

Technology-driven teams help organizations and their employees to concentrate on the work more, rather than indulge in underplay or politics which normally happens in a physical team. This has made and will continue to make teams customer-focused rather than just individual performance-oriented.

Besides the current scenario of virtual teams in the onsite-offshore model, employers are employing the virtual mode even within their organizations. For example, on the one hand, a typical IT organization out-sources work through the onsite-offshore model where offshore and onsite teams coordinate through virtual means, on the other hand, the same IT organization is also encouraging virtual setups within the organization as well. Very soon, even for non-IT organizations, organizational boundaries will not be the only scenario in which virtual teams can operate.

The trend is clearly that of self-managed, strategically responsible, and technology-driven teams. Again with any new trend, you have both advantages and concerns with it. Concerns can be handled only if the advantages outweigh them. Development of technology supported workplaces is the *mantra* for the new age.

Another area where organizations need to work on is developing team managers in such a way that they will move out from the traditional mode into the empowerment mode and aid team transitions. Team managers ought to imbibe new values and principles of operating as a part of being in a team. This means self-managed teams lead to a reasonable amount of investment in team manager training as well.

Organizations are becoming more vigilant in understanding their resources' capabilities, and implementing more sophisticated workforce planning tools to find the best resources for their projects. This in turn leads to more diversity, as a result of which chances of conflict become higher. As more and more organizations restructure to adopt the team model, the need for training in conflict management will continue to grow.

The next level of teamwork is not only going to be the development of a new type of team but also the emergence of a new type of organization, which will operate in a multicultural environment, *seamlessly*.

Peer-based, self-directed, shared space, technology-driven remote teams are a high risk strategy unless organizations are committed, as they require heavy investment in technology as well as in team training. Future trends are all about flattening the pyramid of control, even more. Definitely, these are going to be the in-thing of the corporate world.

12.1 Global Homogeneity—'Multicultural Teams'

With cross-border mobility coupled with advances in technology sweeping the world, it is much easier for people to move from one country to the other, leading to the creation of 'Multicultural teams'.

Sustainable team performance can be achieved, only when team members and their diversity has been successfully adapted to the working practices, corporate culture, and most importantly the cultural differences. Vigilant team managers need to separate out and focus on those differences which are most difficult to handle, and micromanage them until they are eliminated. For example, the IT department of a large multinational software firm I studied, added people from India to a project team that consisted of people from UK. The team manager realized the Indian team was not able to perform as well as its UK counterparts. He immediately decided to micromanage the problem and put in place a cultural training session. At the end of the session, he was able to find the true source of the problem, it was the difference in accent and jargons used, which caused the delays in delivering results.

Smooth interfaces and well instituted hand-offs are a must for smooth communication involving people whose native languages are diverse. A team manager and the diverse elements of his team must strive hard to bring about a culture of mutual respect. Constant dialog facilitated by a diversity consultant creates space for each and every team member on a team. Differences in culture lead to fear of rejection; the only way to efface this fear is through respect for differences. When it comes to language differences, it is always better for all team members to stay away from slang/lingo/jargons, and stick to professional communication.

Active feedback loops are a must for the development of honest rapport in a team. Constant supervisory feedback to team members helps them to reorient themselves to the operational procedures of their team, and prevent the occurrence of communication glitches in the working language.

The two most important factors for building cross-cultural teams are tolerance and cross-cultural awareness. With increased tolerance and awareness, people will fear less and be more open to stepping out of their cultural boundaries in order to adopt new ways of thinking and functioning. The habit of reflecting on one's own culture also helps to realize which things are positive factors and which are the hindering aspects. It is always better to analyze the values, beliefs and assumptions of one's own native culture, before trying to analyze a different culture.

Last but not least, global leadership competencies and skills are very much needed to deal with the challenges of cultural diversity.

All the above shifts in team building are recapped in the Transition Paradigm, next section.

12.2 The Transition Paradigm—'An Organization is Only as Great as its Workforce Is'

Focus is shifting from self-directed work teams
To a network of self-directed work teams,
For generating multiple growth streams.

Table 12.1: The Transition Paradigm

Current Scenario	Future Scenario
Moderately empowered teams	Fully self-managed teams
A mix of physical and virtual teams with more of physical collaboration	A mix of physical and virtual teams with more of virtual teams

(Contd...)

Team manager as team facilitator	A resource of the team itself
Organizations focus on building teams	Focus towards building a 'network of teams'
Project-driven teams	Resource-driven teams
Task-oriented team members	Collaborative colleagues with broader job assignments
Functional Teams	Cross-functional teams
Team building	Seamless system of support
Cross-team collaboration	Cross-boundary collaboration
A mix of project, cross-functional and self-managed teams	Mainly self-managed and self-directed teams

12.3 Challenges—'Overcome Challenges with Commitment'

Commitment at all levels
Is the most crucial element
For a smooth transition, at all levels.

A. Technology Tools

In the immediate future, 'technology teams' will be the key player. The main concern for organizations is that of keeping abreast with modern communication tools. Organization leaders need to rationalize and weigh the pros and cons in inculcating the technology team culture as against the investment in upgrading the technology tools. This decision becomes all the more critical in today's times of economic crisis.

B. Team Manager's Mindset

Organizations need to be mindful of resistance that comes from team managers operating in the traditional style of leadership.

Changing this mindset is required to eliminate ego clashes, as in an SDWT a team manager's role and its dimensions change to a considerable extent, because the power shifts from team managers to teams. For any change in culture, team managers need to be handled first, or else once a team begins operating in a new culture, there will be an endless slew of conflicts. People who are readily willing to accept the non-traditional role need to be trained in the various new responsibilities, which consist of coaching, mentoring and delegation. In short, a new leadership style needs to be evolved and trained for.

A typical team manager's mindset has to undergo changes, just the way it did when the traditional models of conducting business transitioned to adopt team culture. Team managers have to be trained to ease their conversion from a leader to a facilitator, and eventually be a part of their team. This change in mentality is a must for the successful operation of fully self-directed work teams.

C. Behavioral Expectations

Organizations need to come up with foolproof ways of ensuring that teams are able to handle decisions that were previously handled by team managers. Various aspects like conflict resolution, meetings and performance issues will need to be handled in the absence of team managers. How will group consensus be reached without any convening party involved in team dynamics? This is an important question that management needs to address on priority one basis. For this, the management needs to work out new procedures and practices, whereby the new behavioral expectations are streamlined. Even empowerment of teams has to have well demarcated boundaries in order to facilitate collaborative management. Organizations will have to place definitive and traceable guidelines around the process.

There may be individuals, who could find it threatening to work in flat teams, since their contribution is exposed to more number of people and hence more scrutiny. The management needs to instill in them the fact that no one person is responsible for team outcomes, rather collective growth is what is more important and such issues need not be worried about.

D. Virtual Teams

The future of participatory management is virtual teams. The most crucial concern is that of emotional bonding. It is human nature to bond and be loyal to a team that we physically work with, rather than working with a team in the virtual mode. This is one concern that organizations need to address before actually embarking on their program of instituting virtual teams. Also other challenges like trust and tight deadlines need to be taken care of.

Managing virtual diversity is gradually becoming the central theme of the wired world today.

E. Training Needs

Organizations will also need to invest heavily in developing a wide spectrum of skills needed to operate in the collaborative team mode. Apart from the main skills of communication, empathy and cross-training, group facilitation will have to be taken very seriously. Group facilitation will require several levels of training and induction, which in turn requires time, cost and expertise.

Comprehensive training is required, not only for the usual skills of communication and problem-solving, but also it is needed to train teams in management skills. This type of training requires a lot of time and each organization must be willing to invest in it. Teams are required to be equipped with the appropriate tools and methodologies to handle the processes efficiently. Against the traditional approach, this new approach will see teams devoting a higher percentage of their time towards training.

At times, organizations have to hire the expertise of consulting services, which helps them to adapt to changing models of team management.

F. Cultural Problems

The most important issue with virtual teams is that of cultural problems. Due to the diverse pool of resources which come from different cultures, ingrained biases lead to complex interactions. The more the number of people, the more the number of cross-cultural problems. In case of geographically diverse teams, managing timelines and schedules is something that needs to be worked out too. Robust communication procedures have to be in place. Due to the limited face to face communication, it is essential to have the required alternate means of efficient communication. A non-bias steering committee is needed to ensure that all the aspects are as transparent as possible and objective communication is strictly observed.

G. Management Sponsorship

The most important factor for envisioning these trends from the organizational perspective is the management's commitment towards this transition process—whether or not organizations will stick to the emerging models and also let teams involve themselves in multi-level problem-solving. This is one major concern, as most of the times, it is seen that the management does not cooperate later on, and this is the major reason for failure. For these trends to fructify, the management support has to be constant and ongoing. They need to strongly champion this transition.

The only way for an organization to successfully implement these trends is to be clear about their future, and how they are going to manage the transition from the current state to the desired state. Management's non-clarity about this transition definitely generates a cloud of doubt in the employees' minds, and makes them feel uncertain about their futures. They need to know whether they are being eliminated or is this transition a part of improving the organizational status. The top management must provide honest answers to employees' doubts, only then the employees will give their 100 per cent support.

12.4 Advantages of These Trends—'Global Growth All the Way'

A seamless system
Is the gateway to global growth.
Webs of world-wide wisdom
Are being woven by technological growth.

In organizations of the future, there will be marginal bureaucratic pressures. There certainly will be less dependence on higher-level managers, and teams will operate in an absolutely transparent and independent manner.

A. Additional Advantages

The usual advantages of the traditional model will always be there in any team management scenario, apart from the traditional positive aspects, there is another set of plus points—Synergistic process design, reduced operating costs, increased commitment, quicker problem-solving skills and flexible response to changes.

One of the most important advantages is that organizations will be able to manage competition without indulging in huge structural changes.

B. Knowledge Transfer

As teams will be given a larger degree of empowerment, they will benefit from the additional roles that they take up. Broader assignments will always be beneficial to them as they gain additional business process knowledge and add to their domain knowledge reserves, apart from garnering technical know-how. Since cross-functional and cross-boundary teams are on the rise, lucrative knowledge sharing is bound to happen over the wire, thus resulting in instant knowledge sharing.

With increased mobility of information and the global workforce, knowledge and expertise can be shared instantaneously around the world.

C. Talent Pool

Due to the revolution on the technology front, organizations can recruit from a broader base of talent. They not only have unrestricted access to resources from the local market, but are also able to tap remote pools of skills using several online tools. With the cutting edge techniques of communication, retrieving diverse skills is becoming more cost effective. Lack of specialized expertise will no more be a hurdle.

D. Optimum Utilization of Resources

SDWTs formed by the best-fit resources, help in engaging the right people for the right tasks, thereby maximizing resource usage. Having the appropriate team members on a team is the most efficient way of operating. These resources are bound to be 25 to 40 per cent more productive than their conventional counterparts.

As empowerment increases, an increased sense of ownership gets created amongst team members, which in turn improves quality of products and services.

E. Teams in the Cyberspace

This setup generates opportunities for a vast number of specialized resources to work with other talented people from all around the world, which otherwise is not possible in the traditional model. This means more number of brains working on some of the most challenging projects.

Another important aspect is that physically disabled people will also get their due share of employment, thereby increasing the level of seamless economic support.

Global leadership is a distinct advantage of remote teams. It lets organizations to leverage their market value by plugging into such teams, whereby incompetence can be totally eliminated as there is no dearth of talent in this virtually connected world.

Where hierarchical power structures became the buzzword of the 1980s, and team-based culture became the trend in the 1990s, seamless cohesion and teams in a wired world are certainly going to be the operational concept in the immediate future.

12.5 Chapter Recap

1. Several of the fortune 500 organizations have adopted the self-directed team culture. Looking at the quantum leap that these organizations have taken; several small scale firms and midsized organizations are coming out of the task force mode to embrace the self-directed team environment. This paradigm shift is resulting in a slew of advantages—economic, social, and technical.
2. As we move increasingly towards SDWTs, each of us will be expected to play a crucial role in formulating

consensus. As most of the teams, in the near future will be cross-functional and operate on an international basis, they will need to be trained to work with diverse cultures effectively.

3. As technology shatters geographic boundaries, people will need to step out of their limited knowledge boundaries and acquire tech-savvy skills, to keep up with the cutting edge techniques of collaboration.
4. The wired world of self-managed mature units is the key to unparalleled growth and opportunity.

Nothing works like Teamwork.
Happy Teaming!

13

Bonus Bytes

13.1 Case Study—'Pump up the Performance'

13.1.1 Introduction

After the successful implementation of the pilot project, another project at GWRL was selected for applying SDWT paradigm. The following case study was conducted on one such team which was already in the transition process for quite some time. The challenge for any organization that undergoes a culture change is to create and more importantly sustain the conditions that will enhance its teams' impact, and stabilize the new structure at the same time.

13.1.2 Challenges and Approach

Even if a single component of a new culture doesn't integrate well with the others, the potential for collaborative performance is impaired. The out-of-place component in this case study was that there was a conflict between the need for change and need for security as far as new entrants were concerned. Two new members had entered the scene, after the SDWT had been in operation, for almost three months.

As these two members belonged to the traditional setup, they were not so much comfortable with the high engagement and empowerment levels of the team. Although they had a broad experience base and much to contribute, it was their old anchorages that were keeping them from giving their peak performance.

Based on the tips and tools provided in this book, the following measures were taken to set things in order:

1. A reorientation and focus session was held, particularly to address the underlying concerns and problems. This was necessary to eliminate reactive, defensive behaviors from new team members and convey the real messages.
2. Full upfront information was shared with the new entrants so as to enable them to be on the same level of understanding as the others. This was necessary to eliminate any obstacles in understanding and delay in duties due to lack of information.
3. Intensive group dynamics training was given to newcomers, so that they would feel comfortable with intensive communication, which is an integral part of an SDWT.
4. Employee-related goals and performance standards were published, which helped the new members in seeing the advantages of the new setup. It made them realize that it is not just about publishing organizational goals and targets, but also their personal growth will be taken care of.
5. The team manager published his own goals and evaluation standards, and made them available to the team for their feedback at regular intervals. This kind of a technique in a way pushes the team manager to perform consistently. Once the team manager performs consistently, it encourages the team to model his behavior, as they know that their team manager is contributing his efforts for the overall team growth. The new entrants also felt assured that they too have the privilege to give feedback.
6. Regular informal discussions were held with new entrants to identify any gaps or missing elements in their understanding.
7. A comprehensive skills analysis session was held to enable the new members to understand how their unique skills and reorganization of team workflow would go hand in hand.

8. In addition to the above points, a support plan with a person-centered focus was developed to ensure a positive learning experience. While developing this plan, the new members were given all the encouragement to provide inputs to the process.

The above measures gave them the confidence that the management has trust in them, and they are treated with empathy and at par with the rest of the team. The training for new members was tailored to their needs, their inputs and concerns were considered in line with self-directed work principles. By knowing that the plan and all the processes were genuinely focused on their needs, the newly joined members felt confident that they could fully adjust themselves to the current setup and ground rules. There is nothing like face-to-face meetings—time taking initially, but time saving in the long run. The team manager conducted face-to-face sessions for new members to discuss those concerns, which they were not comfortable discussing in the open.

The initial stages of the orientation and induction were conducted under the vigilant supervision of the team manager. As time went by, areas related to the actual work were then handled by colleagues. It was necessary to keep all the six senses of the newcomers stimulated, based on the techniques noted in the Six Senses approach, the newcomers were involved in the work right from day one itself, of course with not much burden. The simple reason for doing so was that we wanted them to feel empowered and involved right from day one, and not feel overburdened with only orientation, induction and a slew of information.

The above measures were operational for a period of two months to ensure flexibility and a people-centric focus. By fully involving each and every team member, we were able to gain unconditional collective buy-in. Only by making sure that the new members don't feel out of place and do not hold any notion of inferiority just because they have joined in later, facilitates more group gains.

13.1.3 Results

Effective induction and constant care of the new inductees has enhanced the team results:

1. The error rate came down visibly.
2. The time devoted to the production of new ideas and products increased.
3. The difference between returns and costs decreased to considerable extent of its initial value.
4. Gradual increase in productivity over a period of six months. Informal feedback of team members suggested that a substantial part of this increase was attributed to the new members' expertise level.

Apart from the above quantitative results, a spectrum of qualitative effects was also experienced:

1. The feeling of confusion was replaced with a sense of confidence in the new members. They learned to constructively challenge the way the things were done, as they now know the importance of constructive collaboration.
2. As the new joiners are convinced that they are truly needed by the team and have an equal say in the decision-making process, they put in more value, thereby adding to the overall commitment level of the team.
3. The above factors and methods have made it less cumbersome to induct new joiners. Instead of refuting the well incorporated ground rules, the new inductees respect and adhere to them, as they have realized that the organization believes in work with minimal supervision and maximization of each team member's performance.

13.1.4 Conclusion

With the proper induction processes in place, new members are easily able to plug into the channel of cohesiveness. Their unique knowledge adds to the process maturity too. Now, the team in question runs its own operations—planning, controlling, executing and handling breakdowns. Now, they run their department as if it were their own business.

13.2 Readiness Worksheets

Team Member Initiative Level

The Team Member Initiative Level worksheet determines the level of enterprising traits and behaviors, which an organization is looking for while developing SDWTs. It determines whether a particular team member is more oriented towards self-development, or believes in contributing to team efforts and finally towards organization. The section to be filled by team managers in consultation with other members, comes into play, either when an existing team is being transitioned to the SDWT setup and based on past team experiences each member's initial level is measured, or when a newly formed SDWT has been in operation for a few weeks and team dynamics data is available to study and analyze faulty team members.

Team Member Name:

How will your initiative / ideas / enterprising attitude benefit yourself:

How will your initiative / ideas / enterprising attitude benefit the team:

How will your initiative / ideas / enterprising attitude benefit the organization:

What according to you are the two most important traits of a self-directed individual:

What according to you are the two most important traits of a self-directed team:

What makes you really excited about your work:

You are good at (strengths, skills, etc.):

Aspects that you want to improve:

To be filled by team manager (based on his observations, other members' feedback about the concerned team member):

Readiness Factor	Self	Team	Organization	Notes
Self-esteem				
Promotion				

(Contd…)

Career enhancement				
Team morale				
Collective knowledge				
Better decision-making at the team level				
Reduce cost and lead time				
Increase profits				
Increase customer satisfaction				

Team Health Checkup

The Team Health Checkup worksheet helps you to gauge a team's health. An SDWT's health is based on its performance level in the areas of team goals, team interaction, and team processes. This worksheet is used at regular intervals, especially in the initial phases of the team development life cycle.

Team Member Name:				
Health Factor	Agree	Strongly Agree	Disagree	Strongly Disagree
Team Processes:				
Each team member is given equal time for process improvement suggestions				
Decision-making has equal representation				
Every team member is mutually accountable to every other team member				

(Contd...)

Constructive conflict is used for the implementation of a solution/decision				
Team Interaction:				
Team members interact frequently off-the-job				
There are no cross-purposes or self-serving agendas				
Team members believe in arriving at consensus through harmonious interaction				
Team interaction is more of cooperation and less of competition				
Soft Skills:				
Team members know each other well				
Relate to one another				
Open and honest with each other				
Rely on one another for a sense of uniqueness and fellowship				
Trust each other				
Team Goals:				
Team members are committed to the team goals				
Team members have internalized the team goals				

Team Manager Readiness Assessment

The Team Manager Readiness Assessment worksheet determines the level of mental readiness of a team manager to take on a new leadership role and style of functioning. It also determines the kind of training needed to bring about the appropriate mentality shift in him. Anonymous responses from team members also gauge the readiness level. The section which is to be filled by team members comes into play, either when an existing team is considered for transition to SDWT, or when a newly formed SDWT is in operation for some time and not performing up to the mark, then in that case, one of the probable causes could be the team manager himself, to cross check this, his readiness level needs to be verified again.

Team Manager Name:				
Views on participative management style:				
To what extent do you lay emphasis on teamwork: (a percentage figure or even a short response)				
To what extent do you think the self-directed team initiative will be a success:				
To what extent do you hold the team accountable for achieving performance goals:				
What are the hindering factors that you foresee:				
Level of tolerance for error:				
Proposed self-reorientation plans:				
The subsequent columns are to be filled by team members.				
Aspect	Never	Mostly	As Expected	Excellent
Visionary:				
Encourages team members to take to new directions				
Links team contributions to the enterprise's goals				
Proactive, global perspective and future-oriented				

(Contd...)

Enterprising spirit:				
Seeks new opportunities of team growth				
Challenges team members to exceed their own limitations				
Promotes team and organization's interests through motivation, strategic thinking and knowledge transfer				
Encourages experimentation and risk taking				
Team Processes:				
Empowers team members to have a collective vision				
Fosters collaboration				
Assesses team performance on a regular basis				
Helps team members to overcome barriers				
Resolves conflicts				
Ensures that team members meet the deadlines				
Possesses cultural sensitivity				
Celebrates team achievements				

(Contd...)

Model Behavior:				
Models the behaviors expected of team members				
Focuses on the problem and not on team members				
Acts and communicates to demonstrate respect and confidence for the team				
Network building:				
Builds relationships at various levels				
Communicates well with the top management regarding team-related aspects				
Encourages team members to forge cross-boundary relationships				
Mentoring skills :				
Helps team members understand their roles and responsibilities				
Gives fair representation to team in decisions that affect their work				
Shares information about the organization's				

(Contd...)

mission, vision, strategies and goals				
Helps team members to diagnose and solve problems				
Helps team members to identify opportunities for improvement in performance areas and processes				

Team Diagnostic

The Team Diagnostic worksheet comes in handy when an organization is contemplating an empowerment strategy; there are a few questions to ask before starting the process. The answers to these questions help to get an idea of the planning required for either setting up a new SDWT or transforming an existing traditional team to an SDWT. In case it's a new initiative, initially there will be no data to analyze; hence this worksheet can be filled up after a lapse of 3-4 weeks of operation of the new team.

Team Member Name:

Describe at least two situations where you did not perform as well as you expected in regards to the dynamics of Communication, Group thinking, Relationships, Collaborative learning:

What pathways did you take to correct the situation and how did you handle the dead ends:

To be filled by team manager (based on his observations, other members' feedback about the concerned team member):

Dynamics	Often	Sometimes	Never	Always
Communication:				
Listens as well as communicates with patience and empathy				

(Contd...)

Clarifies doubts and does not indulge in forming baseless assumptions				
Paraphrases others to enhance better understanding				
Asks appropriate questions				
Group thinking:				
Encourages and motivates colleagues				
Works hard to pull the team out of a problem				
Proposes energy sharing ideas				
Relationships:				
Maintains constructive relationships				
Handles conflicts in an honest manner without any cross-agendas				
Learning skills:				
Has self-awareness				
Encourages team learning				
Proposes techniques for capturing and sharing learning				

(Contd…)

To be filled by team member:
Are your duties free from unnecessary rules and regulations:
To what extent are organizational policies supportive of employee empowerment:
What would you suggest to improve the effectiveness of the team and its processes:
What could the management do to improve the effectiveness of the team and its processes:

Appendix
Team Quotes by Chitra

1. An autonomous team is the key to face competition successfully and it is the sure shot way to scale new heights of corporate glory. It is the nucleus of growth and survival, which propels each organization to an all new level.
2. A self-directed work team is a critical piece of the business growth puzzle, which keeps the business on the rise. It is the answer to the gaps in performance.
3. Laser sharp focus is the *mantra* of competent self-directed teams, which eliminates all the hocus-pocus.
4. In physics there is a basic law, which states 'Energy must exist before matter is formed' in a similar light I say, 'Energy must exist before an SDWT is formed.'
5. Just as well stimulated senses make everyday living worthy, so do they add value to teamwork, phenomenally.
6. Building your self-directed work team means building your business. Team members are no longer mere working robots; they too add value with all zealousness.
7. Inherent creativity of the team needs to be tapped, only then benefits derived will be apt.
8. Human energy is the most valuable intangible asset of an organization, which sets positive change in motion. It is the driving force behind the success of organizations, which in turn creates happy customers in the count of millions.

9. Team processes lead to increased efficiency and effectiveness. Right from the first meeting to the final game they create a network of harmony, ceaseless.
10. Team performance is about managing work, optimizing outcomes and producing team players—the biggest perk of self-directed work teams.
11. A successful team outcome is an amalgamation of integrity, consistency and cohesiveness—which perpetuates opportunities, boundless.
12. Specific feedback reinforces performance, helps to rise above industry benchmark and enhances team conformance.
13. Co-existence is not a choice but a necessity that leads to team rejoice.
14. Valuing each other is the basis of healthy relationships in a self-driven team which creates dynamics, supreme.
15. Team conflicts need to be managed properly in order to leverage the diversity and diffuse the adversity.
16. Value team members for who they are, value team members for what they are, only then organizations become a corporate star.
17. The domain of personal responsibility must be extended to team responsibility in order to ensure fulfillment of collective accountability.
18. Constant coordination eliminates the culture of seeking scapegoats and all undercurrents it filters.
19. Team building is the perfect antidote for dysfunctions, leaving no room for office politics.
20. Results are derived from disciplined choices and disciplined choices are derived from motivated team efforts.
21. Strong personal chemistry aligns resources and maintains team unity, for ages.
22. Motivation leads to action-oriented partnerships. Motivation leads to an upward spiral of super wins.

23. Being self-conscious about its own purpose is what makes a self-directed work team an outstanding team.
24. In knowledge-based organizations SDWTs are the norm, which keep organizations always in a competitive form.
25. Commitment at all levels is the most crucial element for a smooth transition, at all levels.
26. Everyone wants to be a part of a dream team. Only when the right values team leaders impart, will such a team come into being.
27. A seamless system is the gateway to global growth. Webs of world-wide wisdom are being woven by technological growth.